stitch

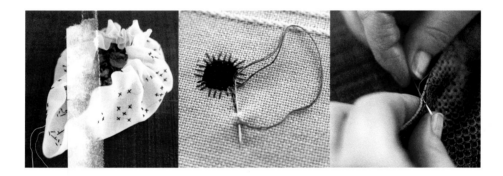

stitch

Designs by
Penny Black

MURDOCH BOOKS

contents

techniques

projects

Introduction

Of the many types of embroidery, cross stitch is the most popular, and is practised by hobby embroiderers worldwide. It is also a very old craft; the earliest known piece of embroidered cloth includes cross stitching, and has been dated to between 200 and 500 AD. It was found in a Coptic tomb in Egypt, where it had been preserved by the dry desert climate.

There are examples of cross stitch from the T'ang dynasty in China (618–906 AD), and cross stitches were an element in Spanish Blackwork, a style of needlework that is believed to have been taken to England by Catherine of Aragon, the Spanish first wife of King Henry VIII. Due to her influence, it became very popular in her adopted home and also spread to other parts of Europe. During this time, folk art incorporating cross stitch was fashionable in Eastern Europe, and was used to decorate all types of household objects with floral and geometric designs. Different regions and countries each had their own styles of cross-stitch embroidery.

Samplers were the beginning of cross stitch as we know it today; the earliest dated sampler known was made in England in 1598. Samplers were so named because they contained samples of a variety of stitches; they were originally made to act as a reference for the stitcher rather than for any decorative purpose. Gradually, samplers developed from their original form into decorative and predominantly cross-stitch versions that told a story, even recorded history, and taught girls how to perform needlework. As letters and numbers usually featured in such samplers, they also helped teach children basic literacy.

The popularity of embroidered designs in Europe spread with the invention of printing in the sixteenth century. The earliest recorded patterns are from a book produced in Germany in 1525. Then, in 1804, the printed form of cross stitch, in which a design is printed onto cloth to be stitched over, took over from the counted form for at least a century.

Since the late 1950s and early 1960s, cross stitch has again become popular as a leisure activity. Many designs are now commercially available; as well as modern designs, there are also charts and patterns depicting traditional motifs and samplers, thus taking cross stitch back to where it came from.

About cross stitch

Cross stitch is simply the formation of a cross by two intersecting straight stitches. The traditional form of cross stitch is worked on evenweave linen (that is, linen in which a measured square has the same number of threads both horizontally and vertically), with the stitches the same in both length and width.

The aim of traditional cross stitch is to create a design or pattern on the background fabric. The background fabric may be totally covered with stitching, or more sparsely covered, depending on the design (unlike tapestry, for example, in which every thread of the canvas is covered). The designs are usually referred to as 'counted' cross stitch; that is, the design is worked from a chart by counting the stitches and rows.

Cross stitch may also be done on fabric that has been commercially printed with a pattern to be stitched over, following a chart that indicates the colours required to complete the design; this is known as stamped cross stitch.

Another type of cross stitch is applied to a background fabric over a type of canvas known as waste canvas. Once the design is finished, each thread of the waste canvas is withdrawn, leaving the cross-stitched design on the background. This technique is useful for doing cross stitch on non-evenweave or otherwise unsuitable fabrics, such as velvet.

The thread used can be of many different types, but a simple rule to follow for traditional cross stitch is that the stitching thread should be of equal thickness to a single warp or weft thread of the fabric being used; this enables the stitches to cover the surface of the background fabric.

In contemporary cross stitch, however, the stitch can be of any size or shape as long as it is made up of two straight lines crossing. This type of cross stitch can be worked on most types of fabric and with most types of thread or yarn; traditional notions of matching the thickness of the thread to that of evenweave linen do not necessarily apply. A contemporary cross-stitch design has few boundaries; here, the stitching becomes a decoration on the surface of the fabric and gives a very different finish to a project than a traditional cross stitch.

Materials and tools

Fabrics

Evenweave fabrics suitable for traditional and contemporary cross stitch are characterized by a weave that has the same number of warp (vertical) and weft (horizontal) threads over a measured square, thus forming a very even grid over which to stitch. Evenweave fabrics are available in many weights, and are categorized by 'thread count'; this relates to the number of threads per inch (2.5 cm). Weaves range from the finest, almost transparent weave of a 55-count linen through to a rustic-looking cloth produced by a 12-count cotton or hessian.

When working traditional cross stitch, it is important to have a smooth, regular surface on which to work; this is the advantage of using evenweave linen, which has been produced specifically for this type of stitching. Contemporary cross stitch, however, can be worked just as easily on a rough or uneven surface as on smooth, even fabrics. Fabrics for contemporary cross stitch can be made of natural fibres or a blend of natural and synthetic fibres, according to the project you are undertaking and its uses. Consider what you are going to make, whether it needs to be laundered, and also the types of thread you will choose to decorate the surface. These threads need to complement the fabric and its uses (and, if the item is to be laundered, they must have the same laundering qualities).

If using fine or gauzy fabrics, as in contemporary or free cross-stitch designs such as the Lavender sachets on page 94, you will probably need to back the fabric with another fabric before stitching, to increase the strength and reduce the show-through of threads from the back of the work.

Although fabrics are traditionally categorized by threads per inch, there are metric equivalents. The metric names of linen relate to the number of threads per centimetre; thus linen 10 has ten threads per centimetre. The following list gives the metric name and its imperial conversion.

linen 8	20 threads per inch
linen 10	25 or 26 threads per inch
linen 11	20 threads per inch
linen 12	30 threads per inch
linen 13	32 threads per inch
linen 14	35 threads per inch
linen 16	40 threads per inch

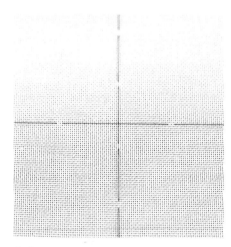

finding centre of fabric Use a contrasting thread and large running stitches to mark the centre.

Other types of fabric

Aida cloth is a cotton or cotton-blend evenweave fabric with a very distinct grid of warp and weft threads. It is available in a wide range of thread counts and colours.

Hessian is similar to old-fashioned sacking. Generally woven from jute fibres, it gives a coarse, rustic appearance to the work. Colours tend to be neutral.

Prairie cloth is an evenweave fabric with an open grid of thick fibres. It is generally 28-count, and is available in a range of colours.

Zweigart Anne (used for the Tablecloth, page 50) is an 18-count evenweave fabric woven with a grid of 12.5 cm (5 in) squares defined by slightly thicker lines in the weave. The grid provides a simple way of defining areas for cross-stitch designs in larger projects such as throw rugs and tablecloths.

Nearly all evenweave fabrics — for example Aida, evenweave linen, prairie cloth and hessian — are available in the form of pre-finished bands. These bands are designed to allow borders of cross stitching to be applied to non-evenweave fabrics.

Organza is a crisp, sheer fabric usually of silk or rayon but sometimes of other synthetic fibres. It gives a touch of opulence to contemporary cross-stitch designs.

Cotton muslin is a light- to medium-weight fabric with a fine, even weave; however, it is not considered an evenweave fabric for cross stitch purposes as the threads are too fine to be counted easily. It is inexpensive and therefore good to use as a lining or stabilizing fabric in embroidery projects.

Preparing fabrics

Before beginning to embroider, you will need to prepare your fabric as follows.

Cut off the selvages, as these shrink at a different rate from the rest of the fabric when it is washed or ironed. Always cut on a straight line, guided by the weave (pulling out a thread will act as a very obvious guide; see page 26).

To prevent the raw edges of the fabric from fraying during handling, finish them by overlocking or overstitching by hand. Alternatively, apply low-tack masking tape over the edges. The tape should be peeled off (or the taped edge cut off if the tape leaves too much stickiness) once the stitching is finished.

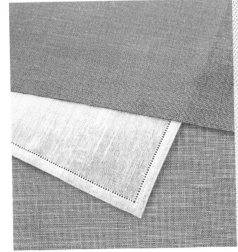

evenweave linen A higher number in the thread count indicates a finer fabric.

other evenweaves As well as linen, cotton and synthetic fabric can be used.

pre-finished Bands of varying widths, and cloths and towels with evenweave panels, are available.

Threads

Threads used for traditional cross stitch and on smooth, evenweave linens and cottons are generally stranded embroidery cottons, smooth linen thread, stranded silk or rayon threads, and pearl cotton. There are other options, too, but it is important to remember when shopping for threads that for traditional stitching a smooth, flat surface finish is the desired look. For contemporary stitching it is the surface decoration that is the aim of the stitching, therefore almost any thread, ribbon or yarn could be used to create the cross on the surface of the fabric.

Stranded thread is, as its name suggests, made up of six strands of thread. It can be used as is, or the loosely twisted strands can be separated (usually singly or into two, three or four strands) to create a finer thread. Remember that when working traditional cross stitch, the embroidery thread should be approximately the same thickness as one thread of the background fabric.

Other threads that can be used are:
Flower thread A dull, almost smooth thread usually made from linen
Medicis or Appleton wool A fine pure wool
Pearl thread A smooth, lustrous cotton thread with a heavy twist
Rayon thread A smooth, shiny synthetic thread
Broder cotton A fine, smooth, lustrous thread

Other than these traditional types of threads, it is possible to use silk ribbons and a large variety of other wools and cottons that are available from specialty embroidery and craft stores.

Colours and threads may be mixed or blended to create a larger variety of effects and colour schemes for your designs. For example, if using stranded threads, you can use two strands of one shade and one strand of another shade to give a variegated effect (as in the Christmas tree picture, page 39).

Remember that a stitch can be made with almost anything you can thread through a needle. This gives you great freedom for experimentation and innovation, especially when creating contemporary designs.

Threads should always be tested on a sample piece of the fabric before starting the actual project; if the result is unsatisfactory, try another type or thickness of thread. Testing the thread is especially advisable if you intend changing the threads and/or fabrics from those suggested in the design. In your eagerness to start your new project it is tempting to skip this step, but it is essential to get these matters right before commencing. A little experimentation at this stage may save a lot of time, money, effort and disappointment in the long run.

Using an embroidery hoop

An embroidery hoop or frame is essential to hold the fabric taut so that it is not distorted during stitching. It is also easier to stitch fabric that is held in a hoop or frame rather than loosely in the hand.

Various types and sizes of hoops and frames are available. The traditional round hoops, as shown in the photograph on page 15, consist of two wooden rings. The fabric to be embroidered is placed over the inner ring (which is sometimes covered with protective fabric tape). The outer ring is then placed over the whole and tightened by means of a screw attachment. Hoops with table-top stands or floor stands are also available.

Embroidery frames are usually made of plastic tubing and are square or rectangular. The fabric is placed over the tubes that form the framework, and half-round pieces are then snapped into place over the top, holding and tightening the fabric.

When placing fabric into an embroidery hoop or frame, adjust it so that the weave is straight, not distorted, and do not pull the fabric drum tight; it should be firm, but still have a little give in it. Never leave the fabric in the hoop for an extended length of time, as this will mark it; remove the fabric from the hoop once your sewing session is over.

Stitch all the parts of the design that fall within the framed area, then undo the frame or hoop and reposition it over the next area to be stitched.

General sewing supplies

As well as the materials and tools specified in the individual projects, you will need general sewing supplies, such as:

Dressmaker's scissors
Paper scissors (paper tends to blunt
    scissors, so do not use the same
    pair for cutting both paper and fabric)
Embroidery scissors
Dressmaker's pins
Needles and machine sewing thread
Tailor's chalk or water-soluble fabric marker
Safety pins
Tape measure
Iron, ironing board and pressing cloth
Rotary cutter and mat (optional)
Sewing machine (optional)
Embroidery hoop or frame (see page 13)

If you wish to chart your own designs, use graph paper; or, if you are very keen, computer software programs are available for this purpose.

Needles

A very important rule in embroidery is that the needle must not create any tension on the thread or the fabric. This means that the thread must be easily passed through the eye of the needle, causing no drag or tension on the thread. The needle should also move easily between the weave of the fabric, without having to be pulled and without leaving a hole in the fabric.

For traditional cross stitch it is suggested that you use a tapestry needle; these are available in many sizes but all have a blunt point. Using a tapestry needle for traditional cross stitch enables you to form stitches easily between the weave of the fabric without piercing the threads of the fabric, as would be likely if using a sharp-pointed sewing needle.

For contemporary cross stitch, however, you could use most types of needles, including sharps, crewel, straw, chenille or beading needles, depending on the nature of the project and the desired effect. It is still vital to remember when choosing a needle that the thread must pass through the eye of the needle easily, and the threaded needle must pass through the fabric easily without leaving a hole.

Most types of needles come in various sizes; the smaller the size number, the larger the needle.

Do not leave needles or pins stuck in your fabric, as they will eventually rust and leave a stain that is almost impossible to remove.

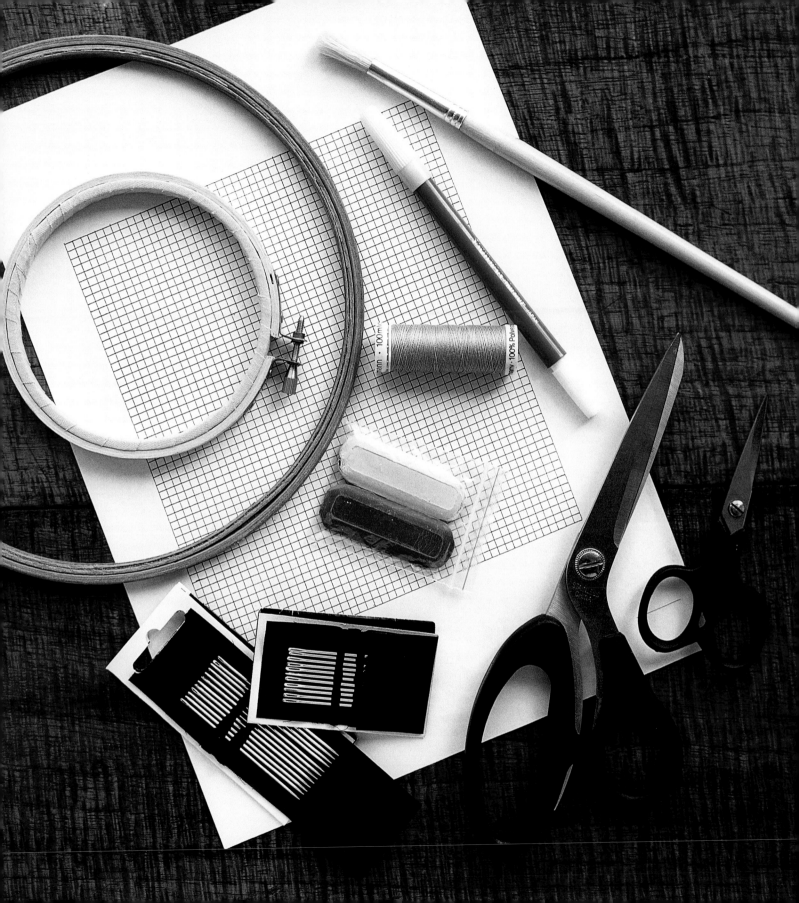

Beginning a line of stitching

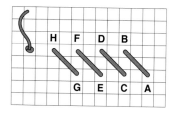

Knot the thread and insert the needle from front to back a few threads away from your starting point. Work the first eight or ten stitches of the design over this thread to anchor it. Once it is secure, cut the knot off and continue stitching as normal.

Stitch library

The following are the principal stitches used in the projects in this book.

Cross stitch

Cross stitch is used for the main body of the design and to fill in patterns.

Cross stitches should be always worked in the same direction, stitching a row of half crosses first, then turning back and completing the crosses. However you choose to work, it is essential that the top diagonals of all crosses lie in the same direction. Cross stitch is generally, but not always, worked over two threads of the fabric.

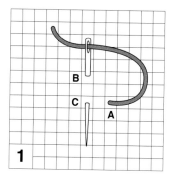

Work the first diagonal from A to B, then bring the needle out at C.

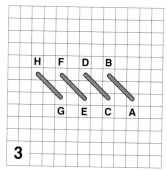

After completing each diagonal stitch, bring the needle through to the front.

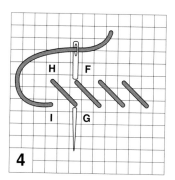

When you have completed all the stitches in a row, it is time to turn.

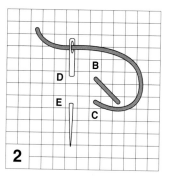

Work the top diagonals in the opposite direction to the bottom.

When the row is finished, move on to the next area.

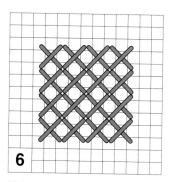

All the top stitches of the crosses should run in the same direction.

Running stitch

Running stitch can be used to form a border.

Bring the needle through the fabric from the wrong side to the right side at A, then take a stitch the desired length at B and come up again at C, the desired length away from B. Repeat to the end of the design.

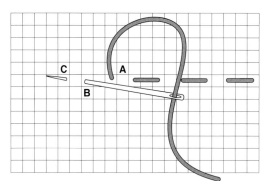

Try to keep your running stitches, as well as the spaces between them, even in length.

Back stitch

Back stitch can be used to outline designs and to form a border.

Bring the needle through the fabric from the wrong side to the right side at A. Insert the needle at B, and come out again at C. Insert the needle at A again and go an equal distance further on, past C. Repeat this movement until you reach the end.

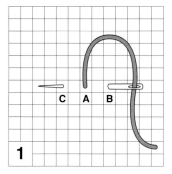

1

The first part of a back stitch is worked backwards.

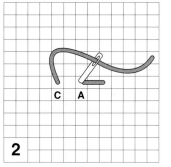

2

The stitches on top of the fabric go backwards; those on the back of the fabric go forwards.

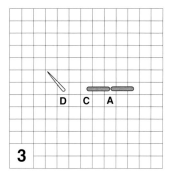

3

Work each stitch over the same number of threads (usually two).

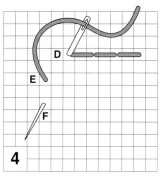

4

Back stitch may be worked in curved lines and around corners.

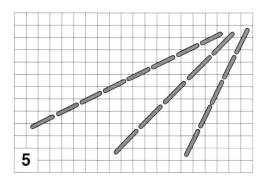

5

When working stitches at an angle, the steepness or shallowness of the line formed depends on how many threads across the needle is brought up at.

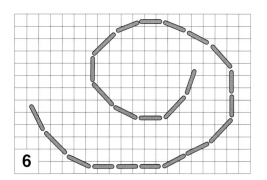

6

Curves can be created by combining horizontal and vertical stitches with those worked at an angle.

How to mitre a corner

On each raw edge of the hem, turn under or overlock the allowance for the first hem, wrong sides together. Press well. At the corner, turn in the second hem if required. Press well. Unfold each corner, then fold up the edge of the fabric so that there is an exact diagonal at the point of the corner. Press.

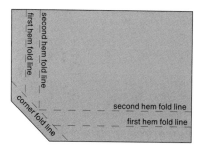

Unfold and trim excess fabric near the diagonal fold, as shown by the broken line.

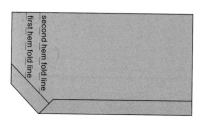

Turn the diagonal over along the pressed line, then fold each side back up along its pressing lines to form a neat mitred corner.

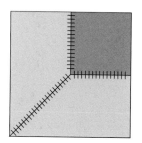

Neatly slipstitch the hem, then overstitch the mitred corners.

Chain stitch

Chain stitch can be used to outline an area or fill a shape. It is also useful as a decorative edging through which two pieces of a project can be joined using whip stitch, as in the Brooch cushion on page 86.

Bring the needle through to the right side of the fabric at the desired starting point. Insert it again in the same place, then come out the required number of threads (here, two) ahead, looping the thread under the needle before pulling it through. To make the next stitch, insert the needle again into the same place and come out as before; loop the thread under the needle before pulling it through. Repeat.

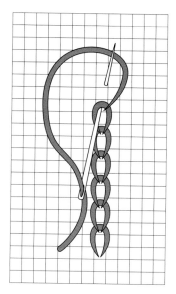

Chain stitch is worked over a consistent number of threads (on evenweave fabrics) or a consistent distance (on other fabrics).

Slip stitch

Slip stitch is used for an almost invisible finish on hems or to close an opening.

First slide the needle through one folded edge, pick up a thread of the other edge of the fabric, then pass the needle through the fold of that edge to the start of the next stitch. Continue making each stitch approximately 3 mm (⅛ in) apart. The aim is to make the stitches as small and invisible as possible, while also holding the two edges firmly together.

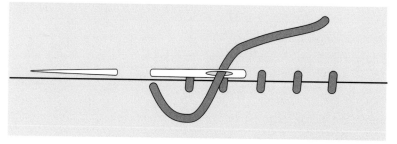

Pass the needle through the fold of the fabric and keep external stitches small.

Blanket stitch

This stitch is often used to finish an edge of fabric, especially on blankets (hence the name), or in place of a machine-neatened edge such as zigzag or overlocking.

Bring the needle through the fabric from front to back at A and come out again at B (generally at the edge of the fabric). Loop the thread under the needle, then pull it firmly. Repeat.

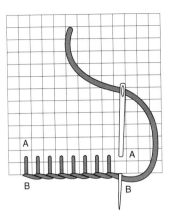

Blanket stitch is shown here worked over one thread in width and two threads in length, although the length and width can be varied to give different effects.

Four-sided stitch

This decorative stitch is always worked in horizontal rows, running with the grain of the fabric. Follow the numbered points illustrated and always pull each stitch tight. Tension is the most important part of this stitch, so don't put your work down in the middle of a row; instead, finish each row. When you come to the end of a row, turn the fabric upside down. Work the next row in the same manner as the first.

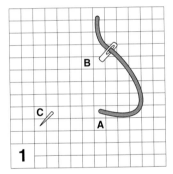

1

Work the first vertical and bring the needle out diagonally opposite.

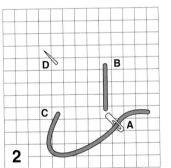

2

Form the bottom side and bring the needle out at the opposite corner.

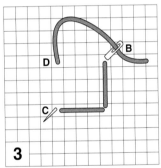

3

Work the top side and bring the needle out again at C.

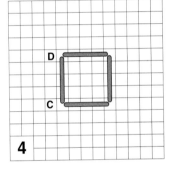

4

The fourth side of the square is also the first side of the next stitch.

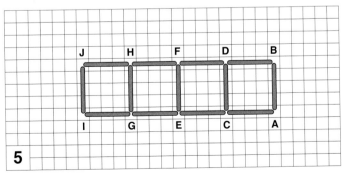

5

Continue along the whole row without stopping your work.

Hem stitching

This is a decorative method of stitching a hem or grouping several threads together. It is worked after the hem has been sewn in place.

Pull out the required number of threads along the stitching line (see page 26), then turn the hem up and sew it in place. Bring the needle through from back to front at A, through the hem. Take the thread to the right; then, pointing the needle towards the left, pass it under the required number of threads from B to C. Pull the thread through, then, with the needle at an angle, insert it at B and bring through to the front of the fabric at D, in line with the point at which the thread came up first.

Repeat to end of work, working around the same number of threads each time, and keeping a constant check on your stitch tension.

Variations

The diagrams below show hem stitching worked over two threads, but it can be worked over more as you desire, so long as the number of threads over which it is worked is kept consistent throughout the piece.

Hem stitching can be worked along one or both sides of the pulled threads, either in mirror image (see Step 4, below) or in a V-effect (see Tissue sachet and makeup purse, page 70).

The threads pulled in hem stitching can be woven in along the 'furrows', from the intersections at the corners to the edges of the fabric, for a neater effect (see page 26).

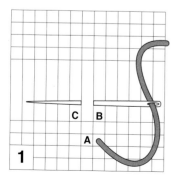

1 Bring the needle through the hem at A, then behind the desired number of threads from B to C.

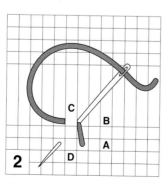

2 Wrap the needle around the threads, then insert it from back to front, bringing it out at D.

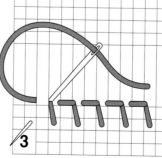

3 Continue along the hem until all stitches are worked.

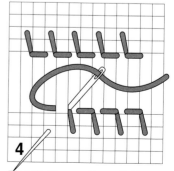

4 For a double row of hem stitching, work the opposite side also.

French knot

A French knot creates a textured and raised effect on the surface you are working.

Bring the needle through the fabric and, holding the thread taut with one hand, wind the thread around the needle twice, then put the needle back into the fabric near the original position. Keeping the loops in place with your thumb, pull the needle through to the wrong side of the work.

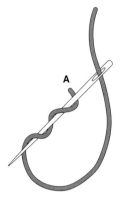 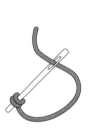

Bring the needle out to the front of the fabric at A, twist the thread around the needle twice, then insert the needle close to A, and pull the thread through to form a firm knot.

Clove hitch knot

To finish your work, use a clove hitch knot.

The knot is worked through the back of the last stitch. Then run the thread under a few stitches (see page 23) and cut it off.

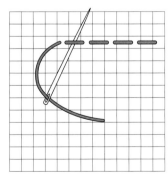 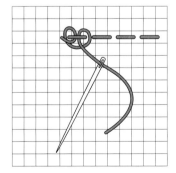

Bring the thread through to the back and through the last stitch.

Work a clove hitch knot as shown to fasten off.

Mounting embroidery

Before framing a piece, you will need to mount it. Cut a piece of heavy card the finished size of the piece, plus about 6 mm (¼ in) added all round for the recess in the frame. Find the centre of the top and bottom, and mark lightly with pencil on the back.

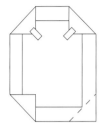

To mount a small, lightweight piece, place the embroidery face down, then centre the cardboard on top of it, matching the pencil marks on the card with the centre line of the design. Fold each corner over and secure with masking tape.

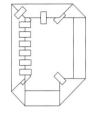

Fold in first one side, then the other, securing firmly with masking tape. Use the weave of the fabric as a guide so that the fabric is not distorted by being pulled unevenly. Neaten the mitred corners, pulling firmly and securing with more tape to give a smooth finish.

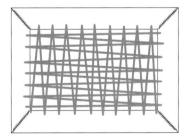

For a heavier or larger piece, fold in the corners as described above, then fold in opposite edges of the fabric and lace across the piece in both directions, using strong thread. Overstitch the mitred corners to secure them.

Resizing designs

The count of the fabric on which you work affects the finished size of the cross-stitch design. For this reason it is important to use the count of fabric specified, or your embroidered design may be bigger or smaller than you wish. However, it is possible to resize a design, as follows:

Count how many squares of the chart the design covers. Multiply the result by the number of threads of fabric covered by each stitch (usually, but not always, two). This is the number of threads of fabric that the finished design requires.

Now divide this number by the number of threads per centimetre or inch of the fabric you intend using. The result will be the finished size of the resized design.

For example, a design worked over two threads of fabric and 40 squares of the chart covers 80 threads. The following would be the size of such a design on a variety of counts of fabric:

28-count: 7.25 cm (2⅞ in)
24-count: 9.2 cm (3⅝ in)
20-count: 10 cm (4 in)
16-count: 12.5 cm (5 in)

Other techniques

Pulling threads

A thread can be pulled to give a guide for a straight cutting line or fold line. To pull a thread, use a needle to tease out the end of one thread of the fabric, near to the cut edge at the desired point. Then continue pulling it out, using the needle to extract the thread as you go.

When beginning a decorative effect such as hem stitching, two to four threads are commonly pulled (see also page 26).

Attaching seed beads

Seed beads are attached with a small half-cross stitch. You will need a beading needle (a very thin, long needle) or a fine sharp needle. Work the first half of the cross stitch, then bring the needle up where the second half of the stitch begins. Pass the needle through the hole in the bead and down again through the fabric where the second half of the stitch ends. Continue cross stitching as normal until the next bead needs to be attached.

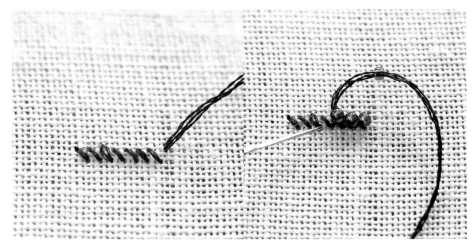

attaching seed beads Work the bottom diagonals of the cross stitches in the usual manner.

attaching seed beads continued Thread beads onto the needle when working the top diagonal.

Making a twisted cord

A twisted cord is an attractive way to embellish or finish a project. Use one or several colours to complement your design. For the projects in this book, stranded or pearl thread is most suitable for a twisted cord, but this technique can also be used with other threads or yarns.

Cut a minimum of four lengths of thread, at least four times the finished length required, and fold in half. Ask another person to hold the two ends while you slip a your finger or pencil through the folded part at the other end. Twist your finger or the pencil and continue twisting until the cord is very tight and starts to twist back onto itself. Walk slowly towards your partner and the cord will continue twisting back onto itself. Run your fingers firmly over the cord to smooth it, then tie a knot in the other end to secure.

Ending a line of stitching

Once a row of stitching or a section of one colour is finished, take the thread to the back of the work and make a clove hitch knot (see page 21). Then run the thread under the back of a few stitches to conceal and secure it (as pictured below), and cut off the excess.

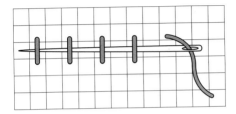

Run thread under the back of the stitching to avoid bulky knots.

twisted cord, step one Fold the threads in half, then twist tightly.

twisted cord, step two Allow the twisted thread to double up on itself. Knot the ends to secure.

twisted cord The cord can be used with, for example, the shoe bag on page 66.

Table runner

From the refectory to the breakfast nook, a runner provides a unifying element to the table setting, whether the meal is a simple sandwich or a six-course banquet. Use a runner refectory style, down the centre of the table, as a mat for condiments, serving dishes and centrepieces; or make matching runners to use across the table instead of placemats.

This simple embroidered and hem-stitched runner can be made in any length to suit your table, and any colour to match your china. The elegant, geometric four-sided stitch will complement any mood, from formal to casual.

Materials
52 x 156 cm (21 x 61½ in) 28-count evenweave linen in ecru
4 skeins DMC stranded embroidery cotton, 3371 (black-brown)
4 skeins DMC stranded embroidery cotton, 840 (medium beige-brown)

Tools
Tapestry needle No 24
Embroidery scissors
General sewing supplies

Notes
The table runner shown is 36 cm (14 in) wide and 140 cm (55 in) long when finished. The dimensions may be changed to suit any size of table, or even reduced to a placemat size. The runner has a 4 cm (1½ in) double hem so that there is no shadow at the hemline. The corners are mitred and the hem is hem stitched with contrasting thread all round the runner. The hem stitching and the four-sided stitching are worked in four strands of DMC stranded embroidery cotton: two strands each of 3371 (black-brown) and 840 (medium beige-brown). This blending of shades gives a subtle variegated effect.

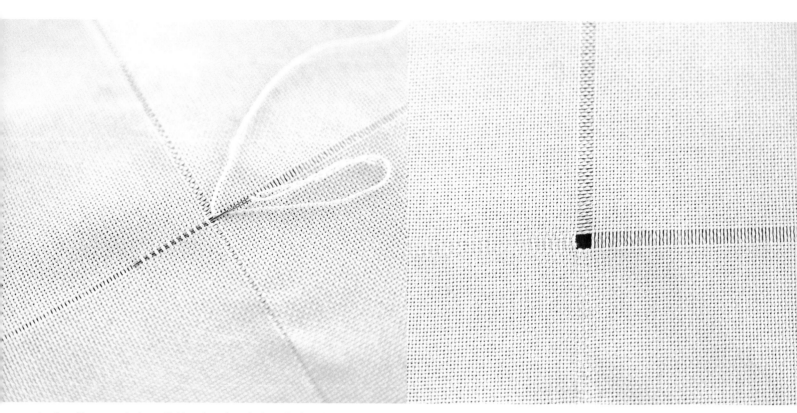

step two To prepare for hem stitching, draw threads along the line of the second hem. From the intersections, weave the thread back along the 'furrow' towards the edge.

ready to hem Showing the corners of the line of threads to be hem stitched, with the threads neatly woven back into the fabric.

Hint

When cutting fabric or folding hems, you might find it helpful to first withdraw a thread along the cutting or fold lines as a guide; this will enable you to fold or cut a very accurate line.

1 If changing the dimensions of the runner, decide on the finished size required and add 8 cm (3¼ in) to each edge. This is the actual size to which the fabric should be cut, including the allowance for a double 4 cm (1½ in) hem. Before cutting, withdraw a thread at the cutting position on all four sides to ensure that you get a perfectly straight line in the evenweave fabric.

2 To prepare for hemming and hem stitching, completely withdraw a thread along the line of the second hem on all four sides. Next, partially withdraw a thread alongside the first, to the point at which the previously withdrawn threads intersect.

Thread this thread into a tapestry needle and weave it back into the fabric along the 'furrow' left by the previously drawn thread, from the intersection to the edge of the fabric. Do this on all four sides.

3 On each side, withdraw one more complete thread, then partially withdraw and weave in one more thread as before.

4 Press the double hem on all four sides (see Hint at left). Following the instructions on page 18, mitre each corner. Slip stitch the hem into place. Once the hem is complete, you are ready to work the hem stitch (see page 20).

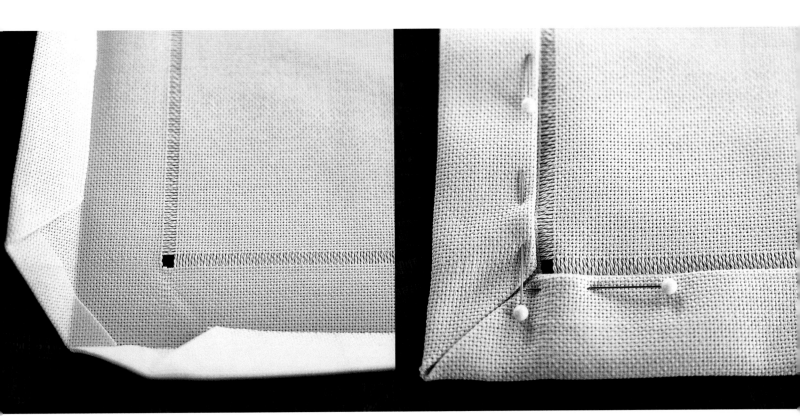

step four Press a 4 cm (1½ in) double hem, then mitre the corners.

step four continued Pin and neatly slip stitch the hem. Once the hem is finished, work the hem stitching.

5 Before beginning the hem stitching, work a small sample to check your tension. When you have a good even tension, start stitching at a corner, working over four threads with each stitch.

6 The four-sided stitch pattern along the sides is worked after the completion of the hem. Measure in 2 cm (¾ in) from the hem-stitched line at each corner to mark the starting point for the embroidery. From this point, work four-sided stitch over four threads for the desired length of the design, parallel to the hem (the length may vary with the size of your table runner). On the table runner shown here, work 21 stitches (about 8 cm/3¼ in) from the corner towards the middle of the short sides of the runner, at all four corners. Then, on the right-hand corner at each end, work 56 stitches (23 cm/9 in) along the long edge. On the left-hand corner, work approximately 100 stitches (42 cm/16½ in) along the long edge.

7 Measure in 2 cm (¾ in) from the outer edge of the first row of hem stitch in each corner to mark the starting point of the inner rows of embroidery. Work as before, stitching 11 stitches (4.5 cm/1¾ in) towards the middle on the short sides and, on the long sides, 26 stitches (11 cm/4¼ in) on the right and 40 stitches (29 cm/11½ in) on the left.

Hint

Try to complete a whole side of hem stitch or a complete row of four-sided stitch before taking a break, as your tension can change slightly if you put your work down for a while.

Cushion covers

These simple cushion covers are an effective way to create a casual, modern pairing, with the design of the first echoed but not exactly replicated in the other. In creamy linen with the sharp contrast of deep navy and cinnamon embroidery and a navy trim, the basic cross-stitched designs create a subtle repetition.

If your sewing skills do not extend to piping and zippers, you can work the embroidery, then send the materials to be professionally assembled at your local sewing supplier or by a dressmaker.

Materials (for each cushion)
50 cm (20 in) square of 28-count evenweave linen in ecru
1 skein cinnamon-coloured silk embroidery thread
1 skein DMC stranded embroidery cotton, 823 (dark navy blue)
40 cm (16 in) cushion insert
50 cm (20 in) square of dark navy cotton velvet for cushion backing: note that 1 m (39 in) of 120 cm (47 in) wide velvet is enough for the backing and piping for two cushions
180 cm (70 in) piping cord
30 cm (12 in) zipper

Tools
Tapestry needle No 24
Sewing machine with zipper foot
General sewing supplies

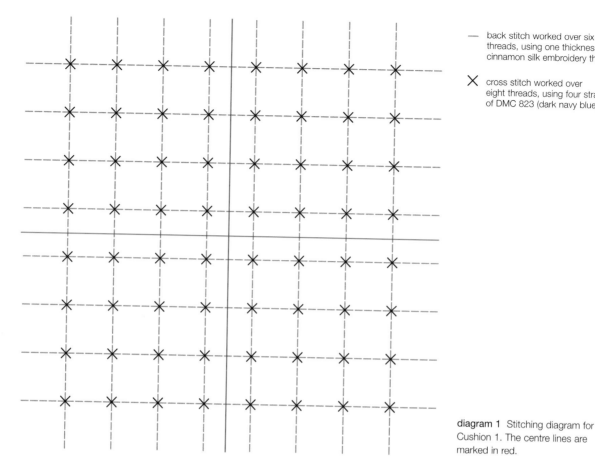

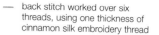

— back stitch worked over six threads, using one thickness of cinnamon silk embroidery thread

X cross stitch worked over eight threads, using four strands of DMC 823 (dark navy blue)

diagram 1 Stitching diagram for Cushion 1. The centre lines are marked in red.

1 To start the embroidery you need to mark the centre of your evenweave linen fabric. An easy way to do this is to fold the square of linen in half, then stitch a row of large running stitches between the two threads at the halfway point. Repeat this at a 90 degree angle: the stitches will cross at the centre of the fabric. Use a contrasting coloured sewing cotton for this stitching and leave the running stitches in place until the project is complete, when they can easily be pulled out.

2 The grids are back stitched in cinnamon silk embroidery thread, with each stitch worked over six threads of the linen. The

smaller grid's squares are 30 threads (five back stitches) wide. To begin stitching, count 15 threads up and 15 threads across from the centre of the fabric. The total grid is nine squares in each direction. You may begin with a knot, or a short tail of thread on the wrong side of the work; be aware that, because of the dark colours used, any thread tail may be visible through the light-coloured linen. Work the entire grid in back stitch before working the cross stitches.

3 The cross stitches are worked over eight threads, with the middle of each cross centred over the junctions of the back-stitched grid, using four strands of the dark

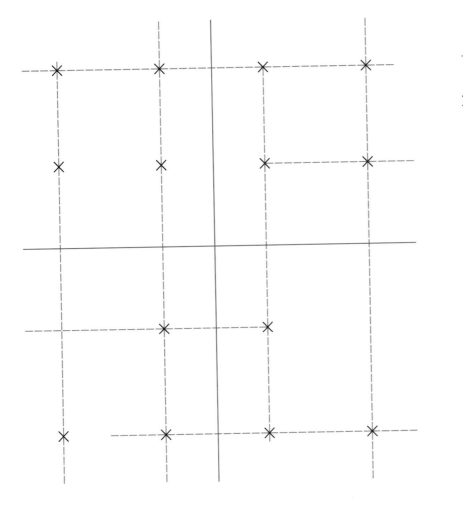

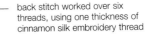

— back stitch worked over six threads, using one thickness of cinnamon silk embroidery thread

✕ cross stitch worked over eight threads, using four strands of DMC 823 (dark navy blue)

diagram 2 Stitching diagram for Cushion 2. The centre lines are marked in red.

navy blue stranded embroidery cotton. Each cross stitch should be started and finished independently (using a clove hitch knot; see page 21), so there is no shadow of thread showing through to the right side of the cushion.

4 The design for the second cushion is not based on a regular grid. From the marked centre, count 36 threads to the left and commence with a line of back stitch at this point, according to Diagram 2, then count 48 threads down and work another line of back stitch at this point. Work the remaining lines of back stitch according to the chart.

5 Note that the lines of the grid continue beyond the main lines in some cases, for up to 30 threads (five back stitches). Work selected lines of the grid in the cinnamon silk thread as before, in back stitch over six threads. Work cross stitches in four strands of dark navy blue embroidery cotton over eight threads at the junctions of some of the squares, as indicated in Diagram 2. Remove the lines of running stitch when you have finished all the embroidery.

6 Make up as instructed at right.

Making up the covers

Trim the edges of the linen so that you have a precise 43 cm (17 in) square, and neaten the edges to prevent fraying. Cut a square of navy velvet the same size. Use the leftover velvet, cut on the bias, to cover the piping cord, and lay the piping between the right sides of the cushion front and back. Stitch around three sides, adding a zipper on the fourth side. If you are not confident with this, take your cushion materials to a professional to be made up.

Apron

The simple embroidery on this apron sets

a tone for finding pleasure in homemaking tasks.

Make the apron in a fine evenweave fabric,

or simply insert a panel of evenweave for the

stitching. Alternatively, work the embroidery

on an evenweave band and attach it to a

homemade or purchased apron. Variegated

embroidery thread adds visual interest to the

cross-stitched border design without the need

to stop and change colours.

Materials

80 x 115 cm (31½ x 45 in) 22-count
   evenweave linen or cotton fabric in natural
2 skeins DMC pearl cotton No 5, 115
   (variegated garnet)
2 m (2 yd) cotton or rayon ribbon 25 mm
   (1 in) wide
Machine sewing thread to match fabric

Tools

Tapestry needle No 22
General sewing supplies

step two Overlock or zigzag the raw edges to prevent fraying, then press the hem up.

step five Work the cross-stitch design according to the chart.

1 Cut the apron from evenweave linen or cotton according to the pattern opposite, making sure the hem of the apron is cut on the true straight grain. (Check this by pulling a thread along the fabric before cutting.) The size can be adjusted by increasing or decreasing the length of the ties. Note that you will need to increase the amount of ribbon required if you do this.

2 After cutting out the apron, it is necessary to neaten the raw edges around the apron to prevent fraying while you work the cross stitch. This can be done by a machine zigzag stitch, with an overlocker, or in blanket stitch by hand.

3 The apron has a 1.5 cm (⅝ in) seam allowance around all side and top edges and an 8 cm (3¼ in) seam allowance at the bottom. At the hemline, press up the hem to give you a starting position for the cross stitch, which is worked above the hemline.

4 Next, mark the centre of the apron: this will match up with the centre of the chart (see page 36). Start your cross stitching at this point, according to the chart.

5 The cross stitches are worked over two threads, using one thickness of DMC pearl cotton No 5 in variegated garnet.

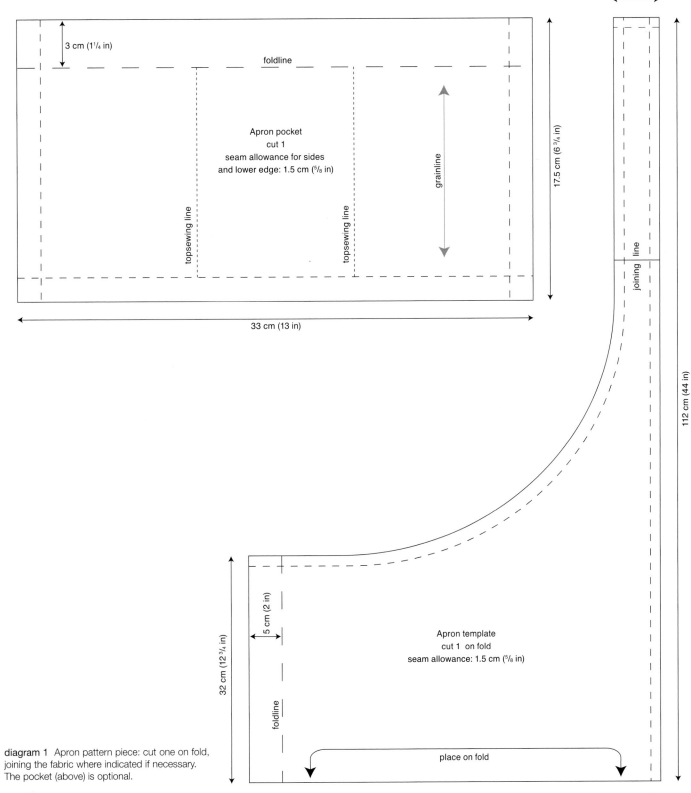

4 cm (1½ in)

3 cm (1¼ in)

foldline

Apron pocket
cut 1
seam allowance for sides
and lower edge: 1.5 cm (⅝ in)

grainline

topsewing line

topsewing line

17.5 cm (6¾ in)

33 cm (13 in)

joining line

112 cm (44 in)

5 cm (2 in)

Apron template
cut 1 on fold
seam allowance: 1.5 cm (⅝ in)

32 cm (12¾ in)

foldline

place on fold

diagram 1 Apron pattern piece: cut one on fold,
joining the fabric where indicated if necessary.
The pocket (above) is optional.

62 cm (24½ in)

stitching chart The red line marks the centre of the design, and indicates where the two charts overlap

Cross stitch worked over two threads, using one thickness of DMC pearl cotton No 5 in variegated garnet

step six Make sure the top diagonals of the cross stitches all go in the same direction.

step nine Add a pocket to the apron. As a variation, the apron can be made in a plain fabric with or without a separate embroidered band.

6 Finish the cross stitches 1.5 cm (⅝ in) from the side edges. This makes it easier to turn over the side hem allowance. Be sure to work all your stitches with the diagonals going in the one direction.

7 After completing the cross stitch, press in the hem allowance around all edges of the apron. Slip stitch or machine stitch in place.

8 Lay the cotton or rayon ribbon across the top edge of the apron on the wrong side, covering the hem allowance. Turn under a small hem at each end of the ribbon and ties, and slip stitch the ribbon to the apron to reinforce the waistline.

9 If you wish to add a pocket to the apron, cut the pattern piece from the remaining fabric. Neaten the raw edges, then press under 1.5 cm (⅝ in) seam allowances on all sides. Centre the pocket on the front of the apron, about 12.5 cm (5 in) from the top edge. Top stitch around the side and bottom edges, about 6 mm (¼ in) from the edge, then stitch along the lines marked on the pattern to divide the pocket into sections.

Christmas tree picture

Celebrate the festive season with this sparkling

embroidery design, combining the rich colours

of traditional Christmas decor with the sheen of

metallic beads and buttons.

For a basic counted-thread cross-stitch pattern

such as this, be sure to start your stitching at the

centre of the chart and the centre of the fabric.

When the embroidery is complete, display your

work in a frame, as pictured, use it to cover

a book or box, or turn it into a wall-hanging.

Materials
45 x 40 cm (17¾ x 16 in) piece of 28-count
    evenweave linen in natural
1 skein DMC stranded embroidery cotton,
    ecru
1 skein DMC stranded embroidery cotton,
    3782 (beige)
1 skein DMC stranded embroidery cotton,
    500 (dark green)
1 skein DMC stranded embroidery cotton,
    3371 (dark brown)
1 skein DMC stranded embroidery cotton,
    3799 (dark grey)
Mill Hill seed beads in colours 03021 (cream),
    03039 (copper), 03037 (mixed metallics),
    02021 (pewter grey)
About 30 extra glass beads approximately
    7 mm (¼ in) diameter in warm natural
    colours
Machine sewing thread to match design
30 cm (12 in) of 6 mm (¼ in) silk ribbon
    to tie gifts

Tools
Tapestry needle No 24
Beading needle

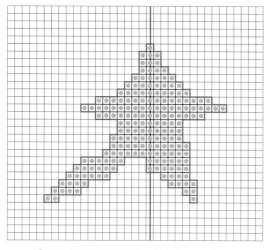

Cross stitch worked over two threads, using two strands of DMC 3782 (beige) and one strand of DMC ecru

Back stitch worked over two threads, using one strand of DMC 3371 (dark brown)

materials The tree design is worked in stranded cotton and embellished with metall seed beads and larger glass beads in warm neutral tones.

stitching charts Stitch the star (above) on top of the tree (opposite), matching the centre lines of the grid (marked in red).

Cross stitch worked over two threads, using two strands of DMC 500 (dark green) and one strand of DMC 3371 (dark brown)

Cross stitch worked over two threads, using three strands of DMC 3371 (dark brown)

Cross stitch worked over two threads, using two strands of DMC 3371 (dark brown) and one strand of DMC 3799 (dark grey)

Tie silk ribbon around gifts at this point

1 The Christmas tree design is worked in cross stitch over two threads in three strands of the stranded cotton.

2 Mark the vertical centre of the fabric with a line of long running stitches in a contrasting thread, as described on page 10.

3 Start cross stitching the design at the star in the centre of the fabric, 8 cm (3¼ in) down from the top edge.

4 Work the star, tree and gifts according to the graphs and thread guides. Match the centre lines and the top and bottom of the two charts.

5 Next, scatter the small Mill Hill beads and the larger beads over the surface of the tree, arranging them in a pleasing design, and stitch into place with a single strand of light-coloured machine sewing thread and a beading needle.

6 Lastly, thread the silk ribbon onto the tapestry needle and tie it around the gifts below the tree.

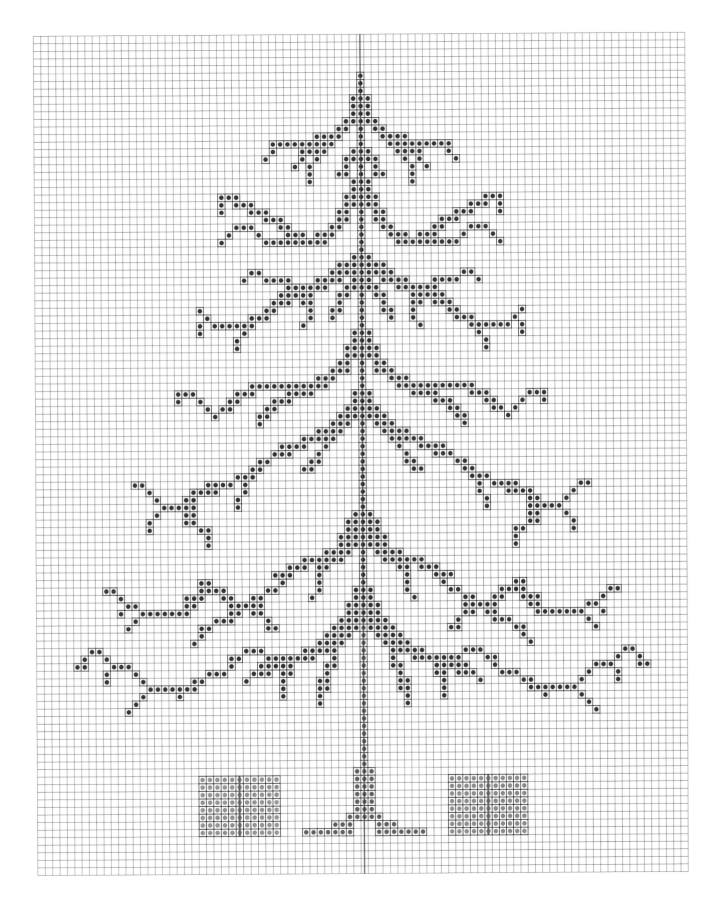

Alphabet

This simple cross-stitch alphabet can be added

to many items, incuding towels, cards, bags,

bell pulls, samplers or bookmarks.

The sample shown is worked on 28-count ecru

linen with DMC stranded embroidery cotton, but

the design can be adapted for other evenweave

fabrics and types of thread.

Materials
Evenweave fabric
Stranded embroidery cotton

Tools
Tapestry needles
Embroidery scissors
General sewing supplies

step one Where possible, work several half-crosses in a straight line before returning and working the upper diagonals of the crosses.

detail The design can be worked in two strands of one colour and one strand of another to give a subtle variegated effect.

1 Using two strands of DMC stranded embroidery cotton in 939 (very dark navy blue) and one strand of 3781 (dark mocha brown), or three strands of the colour of your choice, work cross stitch over two threads of the linen, making sure not to leave any long threads behind to shadow through. Where possible, it is a good idea to work cross stitches in a line, stitching a line of half crosses and then coming back to complete the cross, but it is most important that the top stitches of all the crosses lie in the same direction.

2 If you wish to use the alphabet to make a monogrammed bag, work the desired name on a piece of evenweave linen. Cut out the name, making sure it is centred on the fabric. Remove threads to make a fringe if desired (as shown on the bag pictured on page 42), or hem the patch on all sides, then attach it to the bag using neat hand or machine stitching, or a cross-stitch border. See pages 68–69 for instructions on how to make a lined drawstring bag.

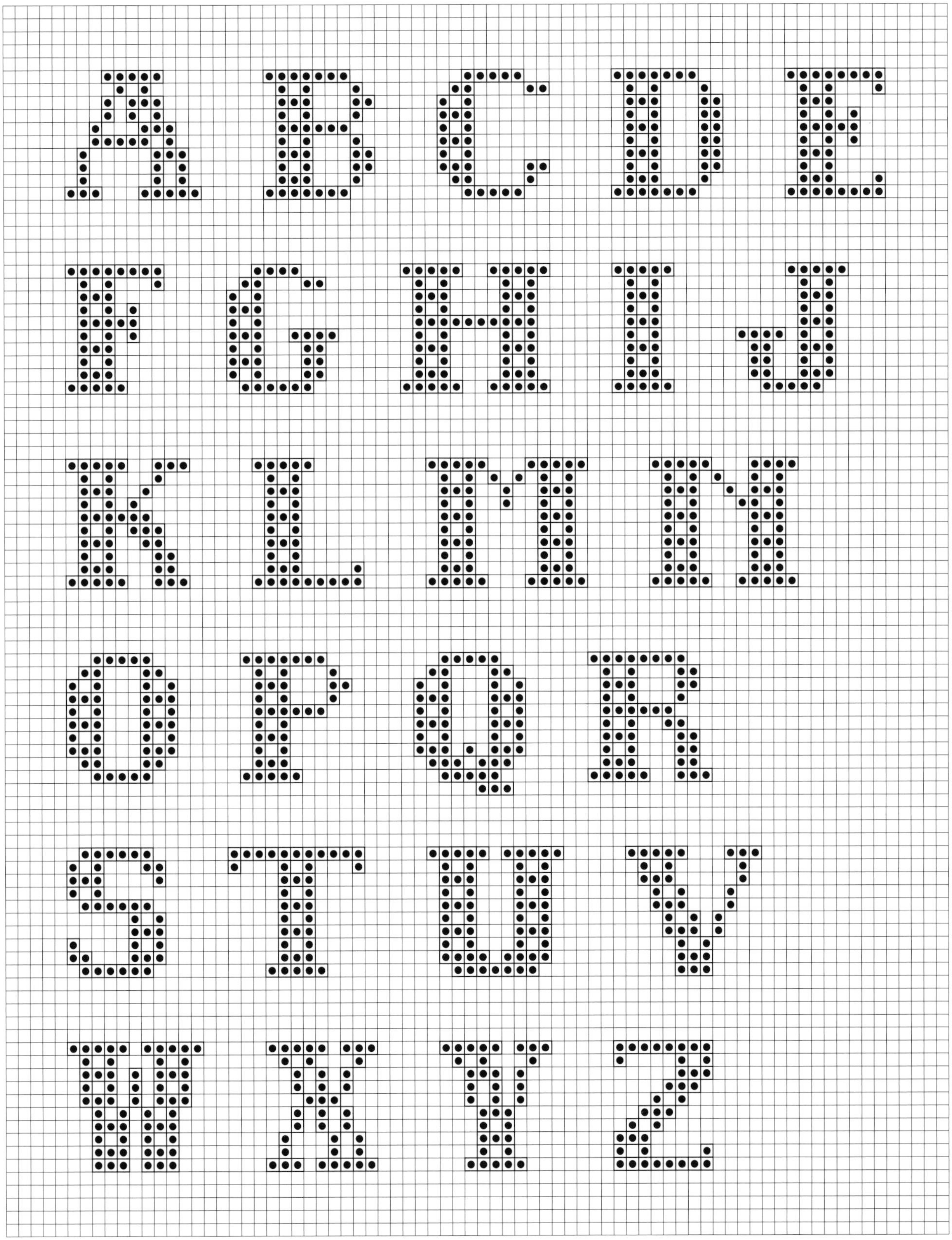

Sheet banding

Crisp cotton bed linen needs little embellishment,

but you can add homemade accents with

hand-embroidered linen bands. Stitch a simple

design in colours that complement your

bedroom's decor and apply the finished band

to the turn-down of your top sheet.

Choose colourfast threads for your embroidery

to ensure that the sheets can be laundered as

usual. You will need to press the band from the

back of the sheet after washing, even if you don't

wish to iron the entire sheet.

Materials
Bed sheet
Evenweave linen banding minimum of 8 cm
   (3¼ in) wide (such as Zweigart Faiden
   100 per cent linen), the width of the bed
   sheet plus 5 cm (2 in) seam allowance
DMC pearl cotton No 8 in white
DMC stranded embroidery cotton, 613
   (very light drab brown)
DMC stranded embroidery cotton, 844 (ultra
   dark brown-grey); note that the number of
   skeins of thread required will depend on the
   width of the sheet banding
Machine sewing thread to match banding

Tools
Tapestry needles Nos 24 (for pearl cotton) and
   26 (for stranded cotton)
Embroidery scissors
General sewing supplies

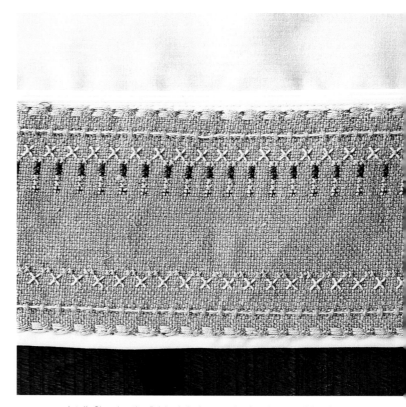

detail Showing the finished design attached to the top of the sheet.

1 To start, work running stitch in one thickness of white pearl cotton, about six threads in from one edge of the banding. Each running stitch goes over five threads and under two.

2 Leave a gap of four threads and work a row of large crosses in one thickness of white pearl cotton. These crosses are worked over four threads and with a four-thread gap between each one. A small upright cross is worked over two threads at the centre of the large cross in two strands of DMC 613 (very light drab brown).

3 Next, work two small crosses over two threads each, between the upper arms of the large crosses, using two strands of DMC 613.

4 Centred above these two crosses, work two crosses vertically over two threads using two strands of DMC 844 (ultra dark brown-grey), then another two using two strands of DMC 613. On top of this column, work one cross in one thickness of white pearl cotton, then superimpose a small upright cross in one strand of DMC 844.

5 Complete the banding with the large and small cross stitches and running stitch border at the top of the band, as indicated

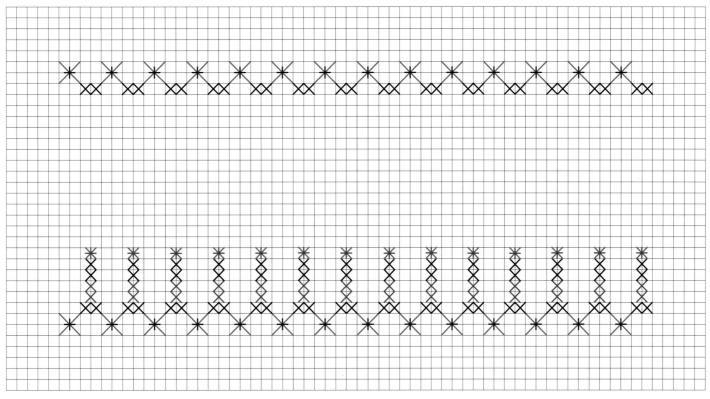

stitching chart See below for the key to the threads used. Repeat the stitch pattern along the whole length of the banding.

in the chart, repeating the design as necessary to embroider the entire band.

6 When the cross stitch is complete, the linen banding can be machine or hand stitched into position along the turn-down of the bed sheet.

Cross stitch worked over four threads, using one thickness of white DMC pearl cotton No 8

Upright cross stitch worked over two threads, using two strands of DMC 613 (very light drab brown)

Cross stitch worked over two threads, using two strands of DMC 613 (very light drab brown)

Cross stitch worked over two threads, using one thickness of white DMC pearl cotton No 8

Upright cross stitch worked over one thread, using one strand of DMC 844 (ultra dark brown-grey)

Cross stitch worked over two threads, using two strands of DMC 844 (ultra dark brown-grey)

Tablecloth

Add extra pleasure to your dining with an elegant
embroidered cloth such as this one. Worked on
evenweave cloth woven with a self-colour grid,
known as Anne cloth, the same design could
easily be worked on any other 18- or 20-count
evenweave fabric. The placement of motifs is
made easier by the grid on the Anne fabric.

The thistle design on the pictured example is
stitched in a subtle mix of dark navy blue and
very light ash grey, but the colour scheme can
easily be changed to suit your preference.

Materials

140 cm (55 in) square of 18-count Zweigart
    Anne evenweave fabric in oatmeal (if
    substituting a different fabric, buy a piece
    as long as it is wide, so that you end up
    with a square)
3 skeins DMC stranded embroidery cotton,
    535 (very light ash grey)
4 skeins DMC stranded embroidery cotton,
    823 (dark navy blue)
Machine sewing thread to match Anne cloth

Tools

Tapestry needle No 24
General sewing supplies

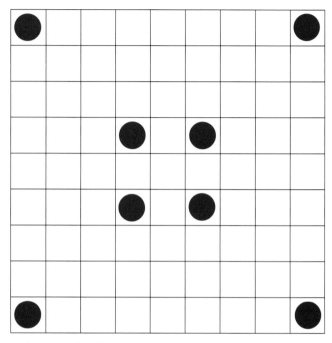

step three The thistle flowers and buds are worked in four strands of navy blue cotton, and the stems and thistle 'beards' in three strands of ash grey cotton.

placement of motifs In the pictured example, the motifs are arranged symmetrically as shown, but they can be placed randomly if you prefer.

1 To begin the tablecloth, it is most important to draw a thread along each edge to find the straight grain. This needs to be at an equal distance from the grid that is woven into the fabric, along all four sides. Press and overlock or machine zigzag a single hem with mitred corners, to prevent fraying while working the cross-stitch.

2 Work cross-stitch motifs in the squares at each corner of the cloth and in four positions at the centre. The cross stitches in this design are worked over two threads of the evenweave fabric, using four strands of DMC 823 (dark navy blue).

3 The back stitches are worked over two threads of the fabric, using three strands of DMC 535 (very light ash grey), as shown in the chart. Be sure to start and finish securely, as this cloth will need to be laundered by hand after each use.

4 Upon completion and after laundering, press only on the wrong side of the embroidered cloth using a pressing cloth.

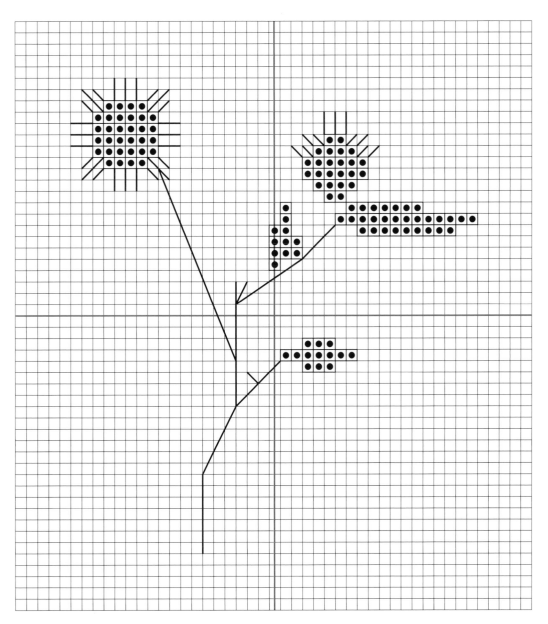

Cross stitch worked over two threads, using four strands of DMC 823 (dark navy blue)

Back stitch worked over two threads, using three strands of DMC 535 (very light ash grey)

Glasses case

Spectacles are delicate and easily damaged,

so a secure, protective case is essential.

There is no reason why such a mundane object

needs to look ordinary, though, and this project

will inspire you to look at other everyday objects

that can be personalized and embellished with

a little embroidery.

The given pattern fits a slim pair of spectacles;

if yours are wider, adjust the size accordingly.

Materials

32-count evenweave linen in ecru
Ecru cotton lining fabric
Ecru machine sewing thread
Small amount of DMC stranded embroidery
    cotton, 3834 (dark grape)
Small amount of DMC stranded embroidery
    cotton, 501 (dark blue green)
2 small bee charms
1 purse clip approximately 6 cm (2⅜ in) wide
30 cm (12 in) of braid approximately 1 cm
    (⅜ in) wide

Tools

Tapestry needle No 24
General sewing supplies

detail The case is lined with cotton fabric and the upper edges of the lining are trimmed with braid.

variation If desired, the case can be worked in the alternative design given opposite, then made up as instructed.

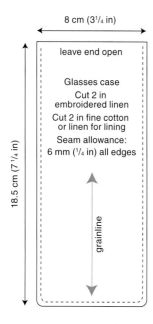

8 cm (3¹/₄ in)

leave end open

Glasses case
Cut 2 in
embroidered linen
Cut 2 in fine cotton
or linen for lining
Seam allowance:
6 mm (¹/₄ in) all edges

18.5 cm (7¹/₄ in)

grainline

1 The cross-stitch design should be worked prior to cutting out the pattern shape, according to the chart provided and using two strands of stranded embroidery cotton.

2 Stitch the back stitch according to the chart, using a single strand of stranded embroidery cotton.

3 Attach the bee charms to the design with a small stitch across the body to hold them flat and in position.

4 Using the patterns provided, cut two shapes in linen fabric and two shapes in lining fabric.

5 Machine stitch the linen, with right sides together, leaving the end open as marked on the pattern. Turn the linen through to the right side and press carefully.

6 Repeat this using the lining fabric, but do not turn it to the right side.

7 Insert the lining into the linen, with wrong sides together, then fold in the seam allowance along the top edges and press flat carefully. Whip stitch the purse clip into place along the open top edges of the case.

8 Hand sew a braid or ribbon trim to the inside upper edge of the purse to complete.

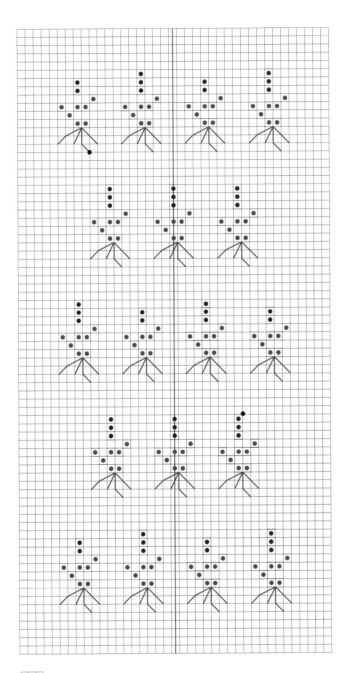

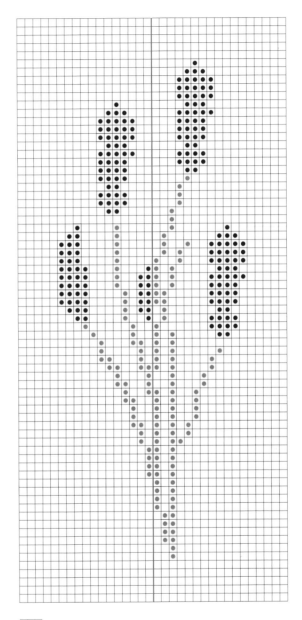

	Cross stitch worked over two threads, using two strands of DMC 3834 (dark grape)
	Cross stitch worked over two threads, using two strands of DMC 501 (dark blue green)
	Back stitch worked over two threads, using one strand of DMC 501 (dark blue green)
	Attachment point for bee charms

| | Cross stitch worked over two threads, using two strands of DMC 3837 (lavender) |
| | Cross stitch worked over two threads, using two strands of DMC 503 (medium blue green) |

Tray cloth and napkin set

Breakfast in bed remains one of those

indulgences we permit ourselves too rarely.

Tempt someone who deserves a relaxing treat

by presenting their meal on a beautifully laid

tray, complete with embroidered table linen for

a touch of luxury.

Any evenweave fabric will do, although choosing

a finer linen cloth will mean the napkin is softer

to the touch and easier to fold when you create

the perfect tray setting.

Materials
32-count evenweave linen in ecru; note that
   the amount required will depend on how
   many placemats and napkins you wish
   to make
Machine sewing thread to match linen
DMC stranded embroidery cotton, 500
   (very dark blue green)
DMC stranded embroidery cotton, 3350
   (ultra dark dusty rose)
DMC stranded embroidery cotton, 3363
   (medium pine green)
DMC stranded embroidery cotton, 3685
   (very dark mauve); note that the number of
   skeins required for each shade will depend
   on how many items you wish to make

Tools
Tapestry needle No 24
General sewing supplies

step two Fold and stitch the hems, firstly drawing a thread along the lines of the hem to provide a crisp and accurate fold line.

step three Scatter several strawberries over the placemat, making a mixture of right-facing and left-facing berries, as shown in the charts opposite.

1 Cut as many mats and napkins as you require to the sizes specified in the patterns opposite.

2 The placemats and napkins have double mitred hems on all sides. To provide a crisp fold line for the hems, draw a thread along the fold lines of each hem on all sides. Then mitre the corners of the placemats and napkins (see page 18). Once the hem is folded, slip stitch it into position. The hems must be completed prior to cross stitching your design.

3 Following the charts provided, stitch the berries as shown, one in one corner of the napkin and one in the lower right-hand corner of the placemat, as indicated on the patterns. Scatter three more berries on the placemat. The pictured example shows three berries stitched around the top right-hand corner. Change the placement of the berries as you wish, but be careful not to stitch them where you would place your dinner plate.

4 Once you have completed the cross stitch and outlines according to the chart, lastly stitch the French knots (see page 21) according to the positions on the chart.

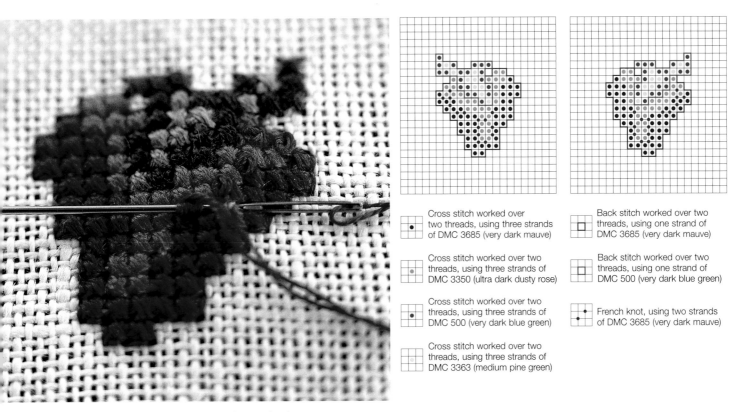

	Cross stitch worked over two threads, using three strands of DMC 3685 (very dark mauve)
	Cross stitch worked over two threads, using three strands of DMC 3350 (ultra dark dusty rose)
	Cross stitch worked over two threads, using three strands of DMC 500 (very dark blue green)
	Cross stitch worked over two threads, using three strands of DMC 3363 (medium pine green)

	Back stitch worked over two threads, using one strand of DMC 3685 (very dark mauve)
	Back stitch worked over two threads, using one strand of DMC 500 (very dark blue green)
	French knot, using two strands of DMC 3685 (very dark mauve)

step four Add French knots for extra dimension to the strawberries.

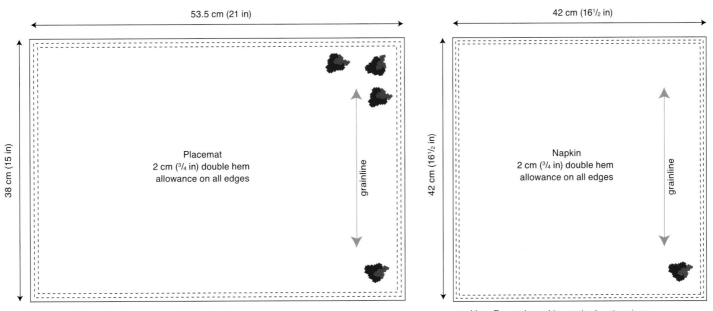

placemat For each placemat required, cut a piece of evenweave linen to the measurements shown.

napkins For each napkin required, cut a piece of evenweave linen to the measurements shown.

Book cover

Here is a great gift for that special someone who has everything: a lovingly embroidered slip cover for a journal, diary or sketchbook. Make it to fit a standard size, or tailor it to a particular book.

The cover can be made to look very different with just a simple change of colours, threads or fabrics. Combine a coarse hessian fabric with thick woollen threads and earthy tones, for example; or use soft linen, pearl cotton embroidery threads and pretty pastels for a traditionally feminine result.

Materials

Book to cover

Evenweave fabric for cover (the pictured example is worked on 24-count linen; see below for instructions on calculating measurements)

Fabric for lining (this can be the same as for the cover, or a contrast fabric)

DMC stranded embroidery cotton, 3371 (black-brown)

DMC stranded embroidery cotton, 3781 (dark mocha brown)

DMC stranded embroidery cotton, 3790 (ultra dark beige-grey)

DMC stranded embroidery cotton, 3782 (light mocha brown)

DMC stranded embroidery cotton, 844 (ultra dark beaver brown)

DMC stranded embroidery cotton, 310 (black)

DMC stranded embroidery cotton, 832 (golden olive)

DMC stranded embroidery cotton, 5282 (metallic gold)

DMC stranded embroidery cotton, ecru

Machine sewing thread to match fabric

Tools

Tapestry needle, No 24

General sewing supplies

Calculating measurements

Measure the height of the book; to this add 2 cm (¾ in) for seams. Measure right around the book from front cover to back; to this measurement add 12 cm (4¾ in), being 2 cm (¾ in) for seam allowances and 5 cm (2 in) at each end for facings. Cut two rectangles using these measurements, one in evenweave fabric and one in lining fabric.

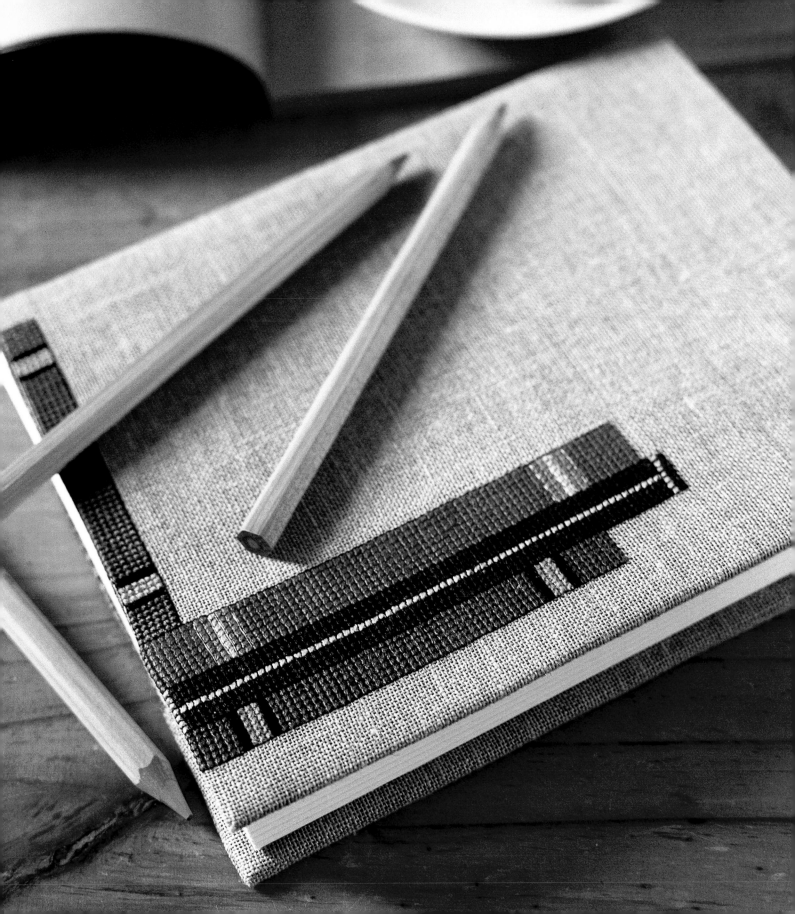

step four Place the cover and lining fabrics with right sides together and machine sew across about 15 cm (6 in) at each end of both long sides.

step four continued Once the cover is turned right side out, slip stitch the lining fabric to the cover fabric to complete the book cover.

Variation

Embroider one or more of the book motifs on a linen or Aida band to create a matching bookmark.

1 Measure the book (see page 62). On the cover fabric, draw a thread 5 cm (2 in) from each short end and 2 cm (¾ in) in from each long edge to mark the fold line for the facing.

2 Begin cross stitching 18 threads in from the right-hand drawn thread and abutting the drawn thread at the lower edge. Work the design according to the chart. Note that the book lying on its side is a repeat of the design for Book 1. Make this book shorter or longer, according to the width of the book you are covering, by adding or deleting rows of cross stitches in DMC 844 (ultra dark beaver brown) in the middle section of the embroidered book's spine.

3 With the right sides of the linen and the lining together, machine sew a 1 cm (⅜ in) seam down each short edge. Turn through and press flat. Fold back a 5 cm (2 in) facing to the wrong side and press.

4 On the long edges, fold the linen back onto itself and machine sew 1 cm (⅜ in) in from the edge for approximately 15 cm (6 in) at all four corners. Turn through to form the cover and facing.

5 Fold in the seam allowance of both cover and lining along the remaining openings. Slip stitch these openings together by hand.

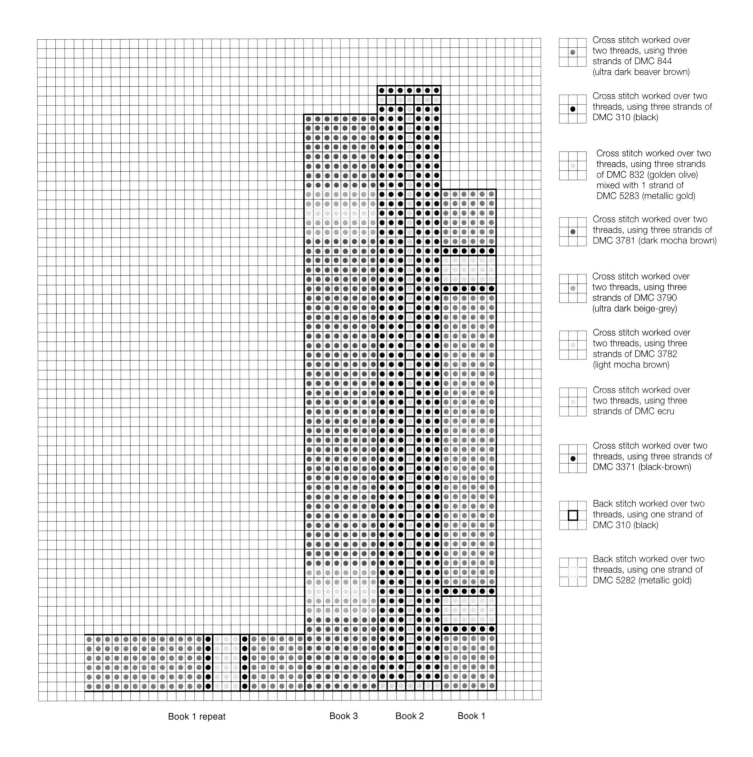

Cross stitch worked over two threads, using three strands of DMC 844 (ultra dark beaver brown)

Cross stitch worked over two threads, using three strands of DMC 310 (black)

Cross stitch worked over two threads, using three strands of DMC 832 (golden olive) mixed with 1 strand of DMC 5283 (metallic gold)

Cross stitch worked over two threads, using three strands of DMC 3781 (dark mocha brown)

Cross stitch worked over two threads, using three strands of DMC 3790 (ultra dark beige-grey)

Cross stitch worked over two threads, using three strands of DMC 3782 (light mocha brown)

Cross stitch worked over two threads, using three strands of DMC ecru

Cross stitch worked over two threads, using three strands of DMC 3371 (black-brown)

Back stitch worked over two threads, using one strand of DMC 310 (black)

Back stitch worked over two threads, using one strand of DMC 5282 (metallic gold)

Book 1 repeat   Book 3   Book 2   Book 1

Shoe bag

Whether you are travelling to a distant destination or just to the office, it's sometimes necessary to carry a change of footwear with you. A practical shoe bag such as this protects the shoes from being scratched and scuffed, and also prevents them from dirtying or damaging other items.

The bag is decorated with a richly beaded motif of an old-fashioned shoe, and embellished with a twisted cord. Make two matching shoe bags as a set for your wardrobe, make a bag to complement your luggage or simply use it as a protective cover for your favourite shoes. Alternatively, the bag, minus the embroidery, could be adapted as a book bag or as storage for craft or other items.

Materials
Evenweave fabric, or other durable, washable
   fabric, for bag
Lightweight fabric, for lining
Machine sewing thread to match
1 skein DMC stranded embroidery cotton,
   939 (very dark navy blue)
1 skein DMC stranded embroidery cotton,
   838 (very dark beige-brown)
1 skein DMC stranded embroidery cotton,
   3799 (very dark pewter grey)
1 skein DMC stranded embroidery cotton,
   5282 (metallic gold)
Gutermann seed beads, 603864 (metallic blue)
Silk thread for drawstring cord

Tools
Crewel embroidery needle
Machine sewing thread
General sewing supplies

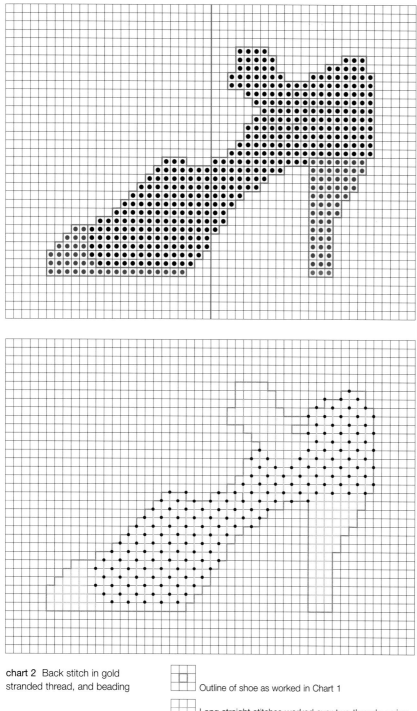

chart 1 Cross stitch and back stitch in stranded embroidery cotton

	Cross stitch worked over two threads, using three strands of DMC 838 (very dark beige-brown)
	Cross stitch worked over two threads, using three strands of DMC 939 (very dark navy blue)
	Cross stitch worked over two threads, using three strands of DMC 3799 (very dark pewter grey)
	Back stitch worked over two threads, using two strands of DMC 3799 (very dark pewter grey)

1 Cut the outer fabric and lining fabric according to the patterns and cutting instructions.

2 On one piece of outer fabric, mark the centre vertically with long running stitches in a contrasting machine sewing thread. Work the cross stitch and back stitch in stranded embroidery cotton using the colours and stitches indicated in Chart 1. Begin the cross stitching along the sole of the shoe, about 9 cm (3½ in) up from the lower edge of the fabric, centring it vertically according to the line on the chart.

3 When all the stitching from Chart 1 is completed, begin stitching from Chart 2. Work the long straight stitches in DMC 5283 (metallic gold) first, and lastly attach the seed beads where indicated.

4 With the right sides of the outer fabric together, machine around two sides (leaving small openings where indicated on Diagram 1 to allow the cord to be threaded through), and across the base. If desired, double-stitch the base for added strength.

5 Fold a hem along the top edge of the outer fabric and press to the wrong side. Turn right side out.

chart 2 Back stitch in gold stranded thread, and beading

	Outline of shoe as worked in Chart 1
	Long straight stitches worked over two threads, using one strand of DMC 5283 (metallic gold)
	Placement points for seed beads, secured with 1 strand of DMC 939 (very dark navy blue)

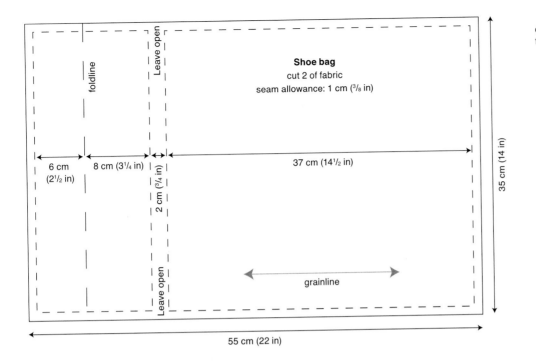

diagram 1 Cut evenweave fabric to the measurements specified

Leave open

foldline

Shoe bag
cut 2 of fabric
seam allowance: 1 cm (³/₈ in)

35 cm (14 in)

6 cm
(2¹/₂ in)

8 cm (3¹/₄ in)

2 cm (³/₄ in)

37 cm (14¹/₂ in)

Leave open

grainline

55 cm (22 in)

diagram 2 Cut lining fabric to the measurements specified

6 Machine sew the lining together in the same way, remembering to leave small openings where indicated on Diagram 1 to allow the cord to be threaded through. Fold and press the hem allowance to the wrong side of the lining, then place the lining inside the shoe bag, with wrong sides together, and pin the two pieces together. Slip stitch the folded top edge of the lining to the facing of the outer fabric.

7 At the hemline, machine sew two parallel rows of stitching to thread the cord through, ensuring that they run on either side of the opening left in the side seams. Thread the cord through this casing and out through the openings in the side seams.

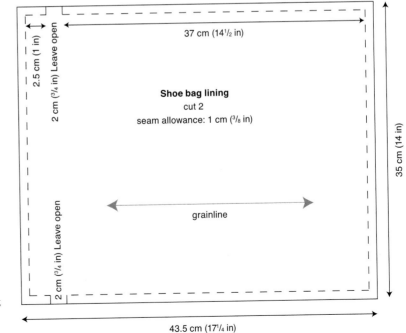

37 cm (14¹/₂ in)

2.5 cm (1 in)

2 cm (³/₄ in) Leave open

Shoe bag lining
cut 2
seam allowance: 1 cm (³/₈ in)

35 cm (14 in)

2 cm (³/₄ in) Leave open

grainline

2 cm (³/₄ in) Leave open

43.5 cm (17¹/₄ in)

Tissue sachet and makeup purse

This prettily embroidered toilette set has a

subdued elegance. The choice of colours for

the evenweave fabric, embroidery, ribbon and

even the lining will change the whole character

of the pieces: the lining shows through where

the threads are withdrawn for the hem stitching,

and you can also change the look by using

a matching or contrasting embroidery thread

and ribbon insertion.

Materials

32 cm (12½ in) square of 28-count evenweave
   linen in ecru (shown opposite) or mid-brown
   evenweave prairie cloth (shown on the
   following pages)
32 cm (12½ in) square of silk lining fabric
   to match the linen or prairie cloth
Stranded embroidery cotton to match
   or contrast with fabric
4 mm (³⁄₁₆ in) silk ribbon for insertion
7 mm (¼ in) clear plastic press stud
Machine sewing thread to match fabric

Tools

Tweezers
Embroidery scissors
Tapestry needle
Straw needle
General sewing supplies

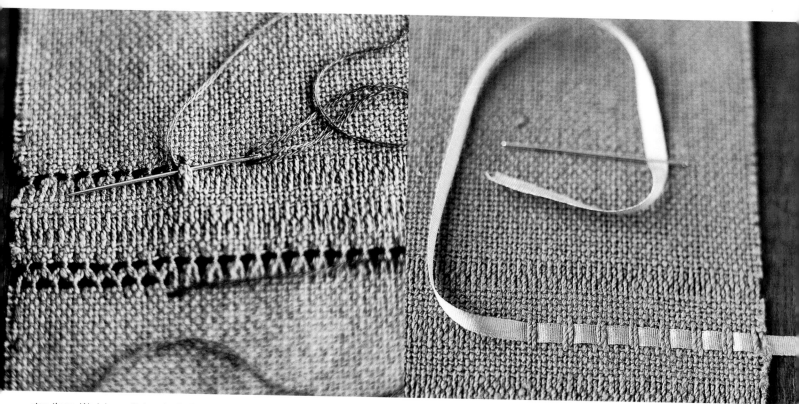

step three Work hem stitch on both sides of the withdrawn threads to form a V pattern.

step four Weave the silk ribbon through the space left by the withdrawn threads.

1 Using the patterns provided, cut one piece of evenweave fabric and one of lining fabric each for the purse and tissue sachet. Mark the fold lines and seam allowances.

2 Withdraw threads using a pair of tweezers, in the following order. For the front flap of the makeup purse, count 10 threads from the hemline of the flap and withdraw six threads; count six threads, then withdraw five threads; count another six threads, then withdraw six threads. For the tissue sachet, count eight threads from the hemline at the top and bottom and withdraw threads in the same arrangement as for the makeup purse flap.

3 Work hem stitch along both edges of the outer rows where threads have been withdrawn. Use two strands of embroidery cotton for this stitching. The hem stitch is worked by grouping four threads together across one side, then on the opposite side grouping two threads from each adjacent group to create the V-shaped effect.

4 Thread the straw needle with silk ribbon and weave the ribbon through the centre section of withdrawn threads, going under two threads, then over four threads. Ensure the ribbon lies flat as you draw it through.

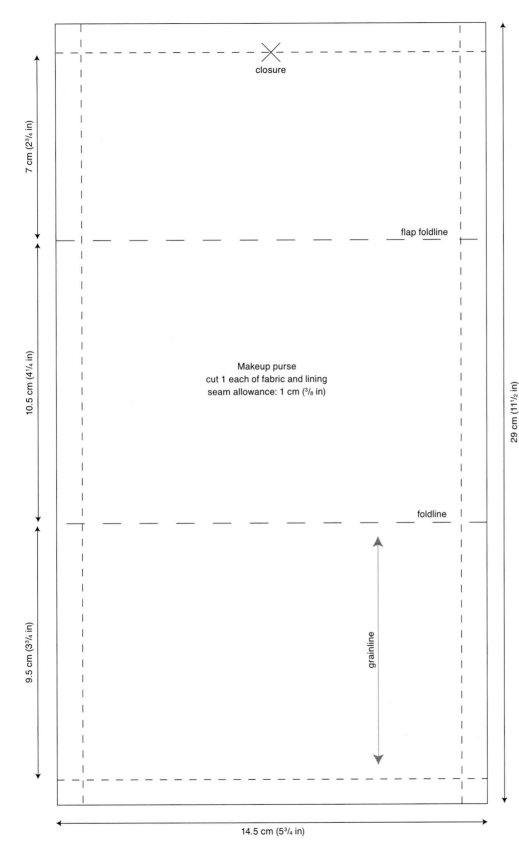

closure

7 cm (2³/₄ in)

flap foldline

Makeup purse
cut 1 each of fabric and lining
seam allowance: 1 cm (³/₈ in)

10.5 cm (4¹/₄ in)

foldline

grainline

9.5 cm (3³/₄ in)

29 cm (11¹/₂ in)

14.5 cm (5³/₄ in)

Storing fabric

When storing fabric, whether embroidered or unworked, it is preferable wherever possible to roll rather than fold it. This is especially important if the work is going to be put away for some time; if the fabric is folded, over time the creases may become hard to remove and will also eventually weaken the fabric.

Roll the fabric with the right side inwards (if you like, roll it around the cardboard core of a roll of plastic wrap or kitchen towel for added support), and then wrap in a clean cotton cloth for extra protection. If you must fold the item — for example, if it is too large to roll — then lay a towel over the right side of the fabric and fold the two up together, as this will prevent creases. Also, make sure that the fabric is occasionally refolded along different lines.

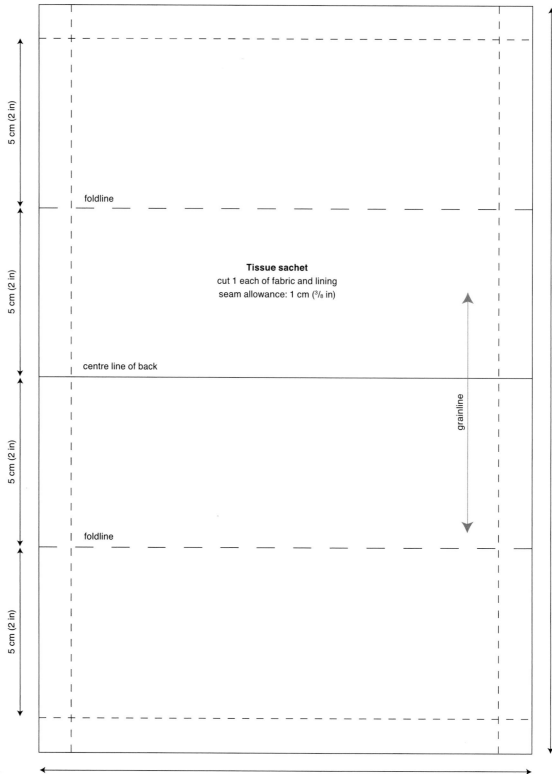

5 cm (2 in)

foldline

5 cm (2 in)

Tissue sachet
cut 1 each of fabric and lining
seam allowance: 1 cm (³/₈ in)

grainline

centre line of back

5 cm (2 in)

foldline

5 cm (2 in)

22 cm (8³/₄ in)

15 cm (6 in)

step four continued Showing one row of double hem stitching completed, the other in progress.

step five Slip stitch the lining to the evenweave fabric.

5 Finger press the seam allowances along the edges of both the linen and lining. For the makeup purse, turn under a slightly bigger hem on the lining so that it sits a millimetre or two inside the edge of the evenweave fabric when the two are placed with wrong sides together. Slip stitch the lining to the evenweave fabric around all sides and press flat from the lining side.

6 For the tissue sachet, finger press the hems at the embroidered ends only. Slip stitch the lining and the evenweave fabric together at the ends, then with right sides together, fold the ends to the middle. Pin, stitch and overlock the side seams.

7 Turn through to the right side and insert a pocket tissue pack.

8 Fold the makeup purse along the lines indicated on the pattern. The shorter end is the front flap with the embroidery on it. Press lightly from the back, using a pressing cloth to protect the fabric and embroidery. Slip stitch the side seams.

9 Attach a clear plastic press stud to the flap and the purse front to close the purse.

Hint

Silk ribbon is available from most embroidery stores in a variety of widths and colours. Its delicate sheen makes it a delight to work with. When withdrawing the threads for the ribbon insertion in this project, ensure that you withdraw enough threads for the ribbon to sit flat without bunching, but not so many that it is not held straight and secure in the weave of the fabric.

Cross stitch cards

Accompanying a gift with a handmade card is a lovely personalized touch. Blank cards are available from craft stores, some embroidery stores and specialty paper stores. The designs shown are worked on evenweave fabric in a variety of threads; you can change the type of thread to achieve a different effect.

Secure the embroidery to the cards with fabric adhesive or double-sided adhesive tape.

Materials

Design 1 (nappy pins)
28-count evenweave linen in ecru
DMC stranded embroidery cotton, 3799 (very dark pewter grey)
DMC stranded embroidery cotton, 3782 (light mocha brown)
DMC stranded embroidery cotton, 816 (garnet)
DMC stranded embroidery cotton, 930 (dark antique blue)

Design 2 (Aztec-style motif)
18-count evenweave linen in stone
DMC Medicis wool, 8102 (medium dark garnet)
DMC Medicis wool, 8306 (dark coffee brown)
DMC Medicis wool, 8307 (dark tawny)

Design 3 (floral)
28-count evenweave linen in natural
DMC broder cotton, 310 (red)

Design 4 (initial)
28-count evenweave linen in natural
The Gentle Art sampler thread, dark chocolate

Tools
Tapestry needle: No 24 for Designs 1, 3 and 4; No 20 for Design 2
Blank cards
Embroidery scissors
Fabric adhesive or double-sided adhesive tape
General sewing supplies

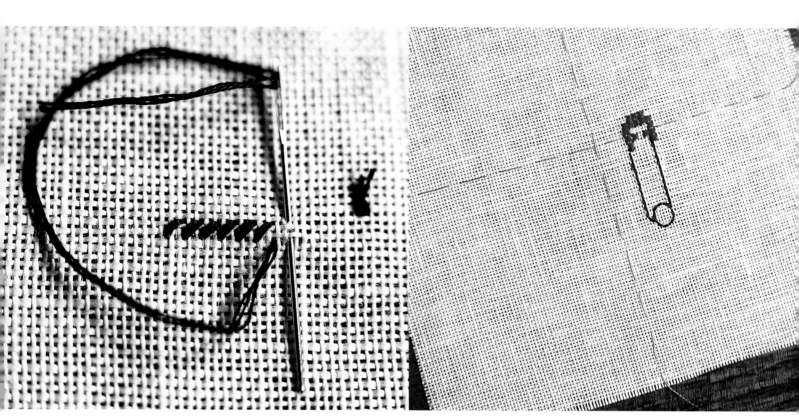

step one Work cross stitch in rows, rather than singly, wherever possible.

step two Mark the centre of the fabric with running stitch to aid in placing the embroidery accurately.

1 The cross stitches and back stitches are both worked over two threads of the fabric. Remember that it is preferable to work rows of crosses where possible, stitching a row of half crosses and then coming back to complete the crosses. Make sure all the top stitches lie in the same direction.

2 Mark the centre of the fabric in both directions with a row of running stitches in a contrasting machine thread. Match the centre of your chosen design (as marked on the charts opposite) to the intersection of the machine threads on the fabric. This allows you to centre the design neatly.

3 Following the charts, work your chosen design, extending it if desired. Start and end threads neatly on the wrong side of the fabric. If working on a pale fabric with much darker threads, ensure that the beginnings and ends of threads will not shadow through to the front of the design.

4 The finished design can be attached to the card using fabric adhesive or double-sided adhesive tape.

DESIGN 1 (NAPPY PINS)

Work the cross stitches for the pin heads in three strands of embroidery cotton, following the chart. Work the back stitch for

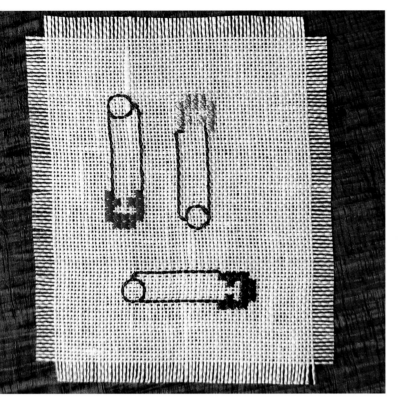

design one Work as many nappy pins as you like for this design.

Caring for work in progress

If you store your work in a wicker or cane basket, line it with woven fabric first to ensure that the ends of the strands don't catch on and pull your fabrics and threads.

Keep work in progress away away from pets and children, and always make sure your hands are clean before you begin embroidering. If you wish, apply talc to smooth your hands before working.

Avoid leaving the needle in the work, as it may rust and cause a mark that will be almost impossible to shift.

Fabric, whether worked or not, should not be stored in plastic bags, as it needs to 'breathe'.

the pin bodies using two strands of embroidery cotton in DMC 3799 (very dark pewter grey), with a No 24 tapestry needle. Work as many pins as you like.

DESIGN 2 (AZTEC-STYLE MOTIF)

Work the cross stitches in two strands of DMC Medicis wool with a No 20 tapestry needle, following the chart. This design can be repeated to create an interesting border.

DESIGN 3 (FLORAL)

Work cross stitches in one thickness of DMC broder cotton 310 (red), with a No 24 tapestry needle. Repeat the pattern as desired to create a border.

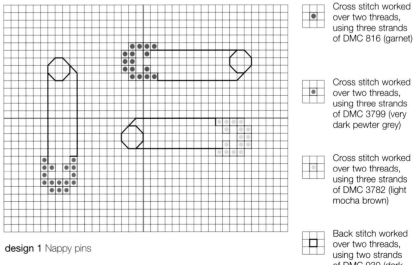

design 1 Nappy pins

	Cross stitch worked over two threads, using three strands of DMC 816 (garnet)
	Cross stitch worked over two threads, using three strands of DMC 3799 (very dark pewter grey)
	Cross stitch worked over two threads, using three strands of DMC 3782 (light mocha brown)
	Back stitch worked over two threads, using two strands of DMC 930 (dark antique blue)

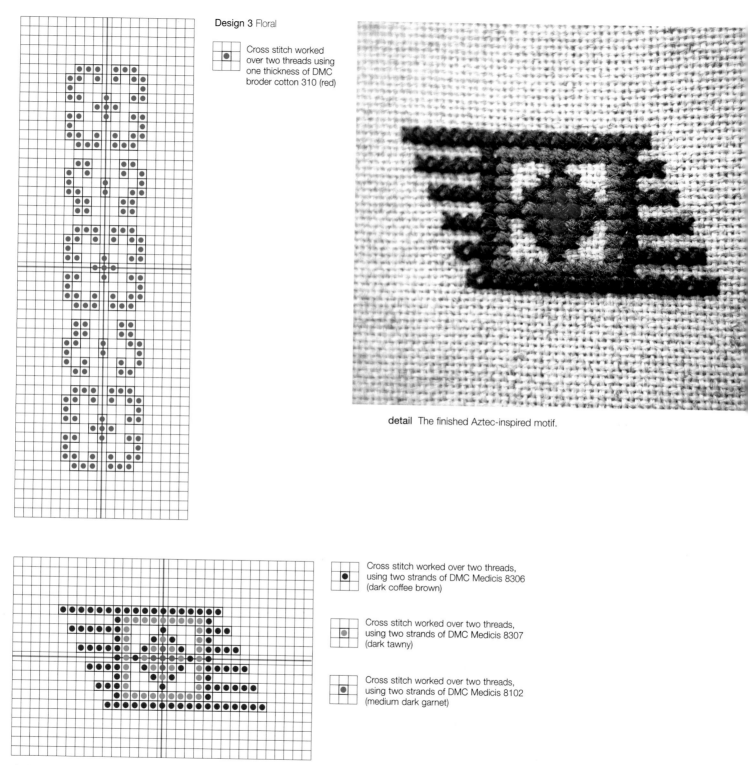

Design 3 Floral

Cross stitch worked over two threads using one thickness of DMC broder cotton 310 (red)

detail The finished Aztec-inspired motif.

Cross stitch worked over two threads, using two strands of DMC Medicis 8306 (dark coffee brown)

Cross stitch worked over two threads, using two strands of DMC Medicis 8307 (dark tawny)

Cross stitch worked over two threads, using two strands of DMC Medicis 8102 (medium dark garnet)

design 2 Aztec-style motif

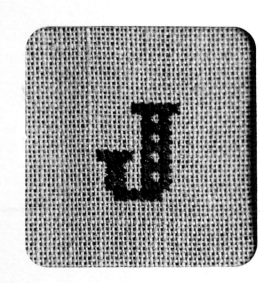

detail The finished floral motif.

detail The finished initial; the full alphabet is on page 45.

DESIGN 4 (INITIAL)

Use three strands of The Gentle Art sampler thread in dark chocolate for cross stitches, working with a No 24 tapestry needle. The design could be expanded to create several initials or an entire name, if desired. For the full alphabet, see page 45.

ASSEMBLY

When the embroidery is complete, select a blank card and trim the embroidered fabric to fit. There are several ways to attach the embroidery to a card: simply fray the edges of the fabric by drawing a few threads, and adhere the embroidery directly to the front of a plain card, or purchase a card with a ready-cut window and adhere the fabric behind the front panel so the embroidery is visible through the window. These cards usually have a flap behind the front cover to hide the back of the fabric.

Buttons

These handmade buttons, embroidered in loose cross stitches and embellished with pretty seed beads, look lovely on a simple garment. Make a set with all buttons the same, or make a mixed set for added interest. Do-it-yourself covered buttons are easy to assemble; kits for them are available from craft and fabric stores.

Materials

Fabric to cover buttons
Voile or interfacing (optional)
Do-it-yourself covered button kit
DMC pearl cotton No 5, ecru
DMC pearl cotton No 5, 840 (medium beige-brown)
Mill Hill seed beads in off-white
Machine sewing thread to match fabric

Tools

Pencil or water-soluble fabric marker
Crewel needles, various sizes
Beading needle and thread
Tack hammer (optional), for assembling buttons

step one Transfer the design onto the covering fabric.

step two Cut out circles of fabric and interfacing.

design 1

design 2

design 3

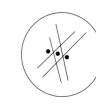

design 4

design 5

Photocopy at increased or reduced size if necessary to ensure that the pattern is the right size for your buttons

1 The designs illustrated at left are stitched on natural linen using DMC pearl cotton No 5 in colours ecru and 840 (medium beige-brown), adding off-white Mill Hill seed beads last. Transfer one or more of the designs onto your fabric using a pencil or water-soluble fabric marker. Ensure that you keep the entire design within a circle the size of the buttons in your kit, and leave enough room between each design to cut the extra fabric required, according to the manufacturer's instructions in the kit.

2 Cut the fabric (and voile or interfacing, if required; see Hint, opposite) according to the instructions provided with the button kit.

step six Work running stitch around the outer edge of the fabric circle.

step seven Gather the fabric at the back of the button and secure the thread.

3 Work loose cross stitches in pearl cotton, according to the design. If you are using more than one colour, work the darker colour first, followed by the lighter one. When starting and finishing threads, take care to do so in a manner that creates a flat result; this will ensure a better-looking button than one with lumpy knots.

4 Attach the beads as desired, using a beading needle and machine sewing thread. Beading thread can also be used.

5 Once the embroidery is complete, follow the manufacturer's instructions to make up the buttons.

6 With a needle and sewing thread, work running stitch about 3 mm (⅛ in) in from the edge of the circle of fabric. Leave the needle and thread attached to the fabric.

7 With the embroidered side of the fabric facing down, place the button in the centre of the circle. Draw up the running stitch to tightly gather the fabric at the back of the button, then secure the thread with a few back stitches. Some button kits have a backing plate: if you need to put pressure on the button to clip the pieces together, use a soft towel or a scrap of quilt batting between the button and the work surface to protect the beads.

Hint

If your fabric is lightweight or pale in colour, you may also need a layer of voile or interfacing behind it to make it opaque and to support the embroidery. If using voile or interfacing, fuse or baste the two layers together before commencing the stitching.

Brooch cushion

Jewelled brooches never seem to go out of fashion. Whether you prefer a classic antique style or a funky art piece in modern materials, having a place to store and display your precious pins is essential.

This small and simple project is perfect to make as a gift for someone you love. The filling of sand and sawdust will help to keep the pins sharp and free of rust. Include some dried lavender flowers in the mix to add a delicate fragrance.

Materials

Two 10 cm (4 in) squares of 24-count evenweave linen in natural
1 skein DMC stranded embroidery cotton, 816 (garnet)
1 skein DMC stranded embroidery cotton, 838 (very dark beige-brown)
Two 10 cm (4 in) squares of cotton lawn
½ cup 50/50 mix of sand and sawdust
Machine sewing thread to match fabric

Tools

Tapestry needle No 24
General sewing supplies
Sewing machine (optional)

step two Work blocks of four cross stitches by four rows.

step six Whip stitch the chain-stitched borders together on three sides.

1 Cut two 10 cm (4 in) squares of evenweave fabric accurately by drawing a thread in both directions at opposite corners to ensure a straight cut.

2 The cross stitches in this design are worked with two strands of stranded embroidery cotton over two threads of the evenweave fabric. The checkerboard blocks consist of four stitches by four rows. The rows of blocks alternate colours; refer to the photograph on page 86 for the colours and the placement of the blocks.

3 Because this is such a small piece, it is not necessary to work the cushion front

design from the centre of the fabric, although this can be done if desired. Start the first block approximately 10 threads (at least 1 cm/⅜ in) from one corner, or locate the centre of the square and stitch the first block there. Work the five-block rows in DMC 816 (garnet) and the four-block alternate rows in 838 (very dark beige-brown), working the brown blocks between the corners of the red ones.

4 When you have completed the checkerboard pattern for the front of the cushion, take the remaining square of evenweave fabric and locate the centre. Work a four-stitch by four-row block in very

step seven Make the filling cushion from cotton lawn. Leave an opening at one side so that the square can be turned right side out.

detail The design on the back of the cushion.

dark beige-brown at the centre, followed by a single border of garnet cross stitches.

5 If necessary, trim the squares to 1 cm (⅜ in) larger than the centred checker-board design. Now work a row of chain stitch around the edges of both front and back squares. Stitch two threads away from the front design and correspondingly for the back. Work chain stitches in three strands of DMC 838, over four threads of the fabric.

6 Finger press the seam allowance to the wrong side, away from the chain stitch. Hold the front and back squares with wrong sides together and the chain stitch rows

aligned. Whip stitch the two rows of chain stitch together, using three strands of very dark beige-brown embroidery thread, until you have joined three sides of the squares.

7 Make the filling cushion of cotton lawn. With right sides together, stitch the squares of lawn together around the edges, leaving a small gap for turning. Clip the corners, then turn the square through to the right side. Fill with the sand and sawdust mix, then slip stitch to close the remaining seam. Insert into the cushion.

8 Whip stitch the remaining side of the brooch cushion, securing with a clove hitch.

Hint

These colours and the block sizes can be altered as desired: try an alternate design of five stitches by five rows in a checkerboard pattern using hand-dyed variegated cotton thread to create the colour change rather than two different solid-colour threads.

Bookmarks

Embroidered bookmarks combine the pretty with the practical. Their small size makes them a quick, easy and inexpensive project. Use woven bands of evenweave fabric, as these have a flat, decorative edge finish: a hem might cause excess bulk that will ruin the binding of the book. For the same reason, do not use knots to finish your threads on the back of the fabric, but run the ends of the thread under the stitching to keep the work as flat as possible.

For each bookmark, you will need 40 cm (16 in) of banding and pearl cotton or stranded embroidery cotton (this is a useful project for using up remnants of thread from other projects). Use the fabrics and threads listed, or experiment with other combinations.

Materials

40 cm (16 in) of 5 cm (2 in) hessian band
DMC pearl cotton No 5, 304 (China red)
or
40 cm (16 in) of 5 cm (2 in) Aida band
DMC stranded embroidery thread, 839 (dark beige-brown) and 840 (medium beige-brown)
or
40 cm (16 in) of 4 cm (1½ in) linen band
DMC stranded embroidery thread, 115 (variegated garnet)

Sewing thread to match fabric (optional)

Tools

Water-soluble fabric marker
Tapestry needles

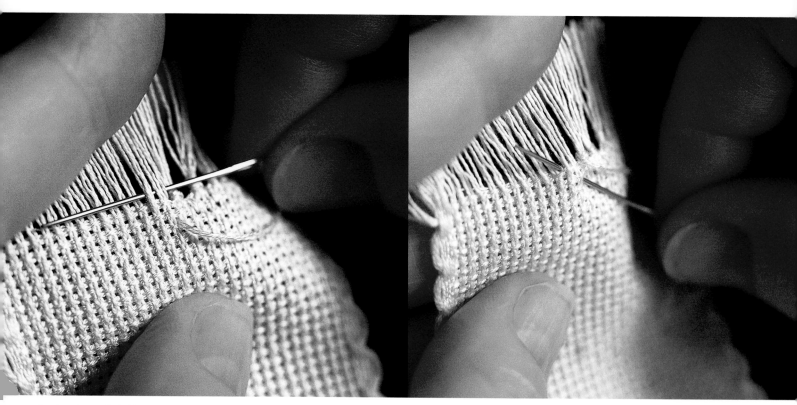

step two, hem stitch Use a matching or contrasting thread for the hem stitching, depending on the effect desired.

step two, hem stitch continued Bring the needle up after a group of threads.

Hint

A frame or hoop can still be used with pieces of fabric (such as evenweave or other bands, as in this project) that are smaller than the hoop. You will need fabric oddments of a similar weight. Cut four pieces to a size that will fit both the item to be embroidered and the frame or hoop, and baste them to each side of the embroidery fabric. Then stretch it in the hoop in the usual way.

1 Fray the bookmark for about 1 cm (⅜ in) at each end, ready to hem stitch.

2 The hem stitching (see page 20) can be done in a matching sewing thread (so it cannot be seen) or the embroidery thread that you are using for the cross stitch; or use the thread that you have withdrawn from the fabric for a slightly more visible effect than when using machine thread.

3 Using a water-soluble fabric marker, mark the placement points for the dots onto the bookmark. In the pictured examples, the dots are randomly placed. On the linen and Aida bands, the stitch groups are more dense at one end, gradually thinning out towards the other end. On the hessian band, the stitches are evenly distributed throughout. If you prefer a more even arrangement of stitch groups, mark the dots accordingly.

HESSIAN BAND

On the hessian band, work cross stitches over four threads in pearl cotton No 5. The unevenness of the weave will cause the stitches to vary in size, giving a casual look. Work some of the stitches in two thicknesses of thread and others in a single thickness to give a varied effect.

embroidery Work groups of cross stitches over the water-soluble fabric marker dots.

These examples are worked on bands of (from left) hessian, Aida and linen, with stitches in stranded cotton or pearl cotton placed randomly.

AIDA BAND

On the Aida, work stitches over two threads using three strands of DMC stranded embroidery cotton. Two charts are given for the stitch groups; the bookmark shown in the centre of the above right photograph uses the stitch grouping shown in Chart 1. Chart 2 is given as an alternative; this design is shown in the step photograph for Step 4, above. Work some of the stitch groups in DMC 839 (dark beige-brown) and others in DMC 840 (medium beige-brown).

LINEN BAND

On the linen, work stitches over two threads using two strands of stranded

embroidery cotton, in either of the stitch patterns in Charts 1 and 2. Using a variegated cotton such as the one in the pictured example will give a gradation of colour without the need to change threads.

chart 1

chart 2 Alternative design

Lavender sachets

The fresh scent of lavender will permeate your wardrobe and your clothing when you use these aromatic sachets. As well as lavender, you can include herbs such as mint and rosemary to help repel moths and other destructive insects.

Silk organza has a lovely crisp finish and the translucency required for this design, while a muslin lining keeps the pot pourri from seeping out and staining your clothing. Hang the sachet over the hook of a coathanger, tie it around the clothes rail in your wardrobe, or place it in your lingerie drawer.

Alternatively, the sachet can be filled with dried culinary herbs and hung in the kitchen or pantry.

Materials (for each hanger)
40 cm (16 in) square silk organza
40 cm (16 in) square cotton muslin
DMC pearl cotton No 5 *or* DMC stranded
  embroidery cotton
Dried herbs, dried lavender, dried rose petals
  or pot pourri, for filling
1 m (1 yd) of 6 mm (¼ in) grosgrain ribbon
  or silk organza ribbon for ties

Tools
Pencil
Compass
Water-soluble fabric marker
Crewel embroidery needle
Embroidery hoop

step two Using a water-soluble marker pen, mark dots all over the inner circle on the organza fabric, to show the placement points for the groups of cross stitches.

step three Work groups of five cross stitches over the marked dots, stitching through both layers of fabric. Do not extend the stitching beyond the inner circle.

Hint

The finished silk organza circles need to be at least 30–35 cm (12–14 in) in diameter. If you wish to make smaller hangers than the size given at right, remember to keep the stitches at least 15–20 cm (6–8 in) from the edges of the fabric to allow for a 10 cm (4 in) ruffle when the organza is drawn up.

1 Using a pencil and compass (or dinner plates of the correct size), mark two concentric circles, 22 cm (8½ in) and 36 cm (14¼ in) in diameter, on the organza fabric. (If you wish to make smaller hangers, see the hint at left.) Do not cut out the circles until after all the cross stitching has been worked on the organza, so that the raw edges of the circle remain crisp.

2 Using a water-soluble fabric marker, mark placement points for groups of cross stitches (see chart) all over the centre of the organza fabric. Do not extend the placement points beyond the inner circle. Note that towards the outer edge of the circle, you will need to mark partial groups of stitches (see the photograph above) to fit the design neatly into the circle.

3 Lay the organza over the muslin and place in an embroidery hoop. Work the cross stitches through both layers, using one thickness of pearl cotton or two strands of stranded embroidery cotton. After each group of stitches is completed, the thread should be fastened off to minimize shadows of threads behind the translucent fabrics.

4 When you have completed all the cross stitches, cut out both layers of fabric into a circle. If you have resized the hanger,

step five Pile pot pourri into the centre of the circle, then draw up the running stitch threads to form a neat ball.

step five continued Finish the hanger with a ribbon bow.

remember that the finished circle needs to be at least 10 cm (4 in) wider than the stitched area. In matching machine thread, work medium-length running stitches around the line of the inner circle. Do not fasten off.

5 Place the fabric circle face down and pile pot pourri in the centre. Draw up the edges of the fabric using the ends of the running stitch, ensuring the ball is well filled with pot pourri, then tie off and trim the threads. Decorate with a ribbon bow to finish.

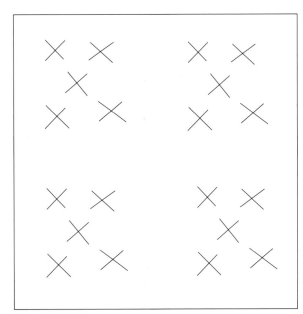

chart 1 Repeat these groups of cross stitches all over the marked inner circle of the fabric.

Curtain

A lightweight curtain admits subtle light through a window. The shadowy shapes of simple stitched motifs on this curtain add a touch of embroidery magic to a plain fabric drop.

This design is made up of diagonal and upright crosses on top of each other, with loosely carried threads on the reverse adding depth to the shadow-work effect. This is a simple but effective way to dress up a purchased ready-hemmed curtain.

Materials

Ready-made cotton voile or muslin curtain in white or ecru
DMC stranded embroidery cotton, 317 (pewter grey)
DMC stranded embroidery cotton, 318 (light steel grey)
DMC stranded embroidery cotton, 762 (very light pearl grey)

Tools

Embroidery hoop
Crewel embroidery needles
Water-soluble fabric marker
General sewing supplies

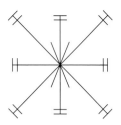

small star design (top row)

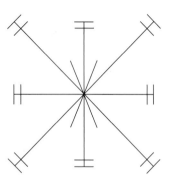

medium star design (middle row)

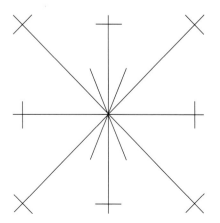

large star design (bottom row)

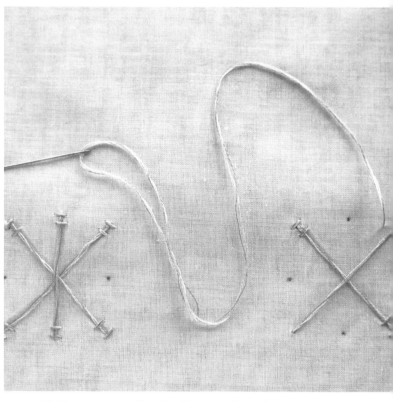

stitching in progress Work the stitches over the marker-pen dots.

1 Trace the stars at left onto the curtain using a water-soluble fabric marker. Following the curtain layout chart opposite, repeat the stars across the width of the curtain, working from the centre out. You can increase the spacing between rows as desired, and increase the number of rows in the design if you have a larger curtain.

2 Place the section of curtain to be stitched into an embroidery hoop. Be careful to start and finish each pattern securely with a clove hitch knot (see page 21). There will be some show-through of the threads at the back of the fabric; this is intentional and adds a soft, shadowy effect.

3 The bottom row of stars is stitched with one strand of DMC 317 (pewter grey) combined with two strands of DMC 762 (very light pearl grey).

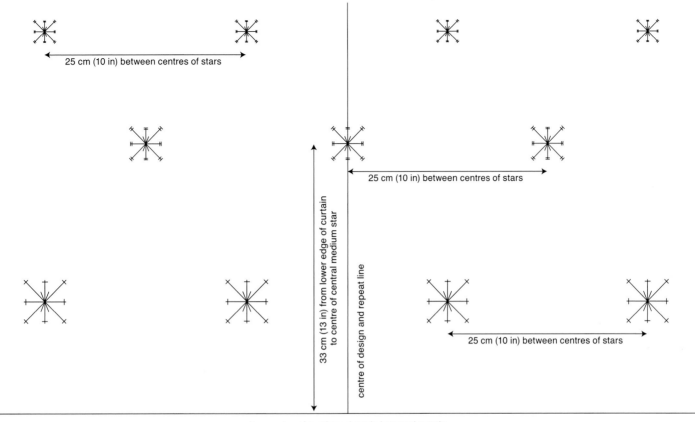

25 cm (10 in) between centres of stars

25 cm (10 in) between centres of stars

25 cm (10 in) between centres of stars

33 cm (13 in) from lower edge of curtain to centre of central medium star

centre of design and repeat line

curtain layout

lower edge of purchased ready-hemmed curtain

4 The middle row of stars is stitched with one strand of 762 (very light pearl grey) combined with two strands of 318 (light steel grey).

5 The top row of stars is stitched with one strand of 318 (light steel grey) combined with two strands of 762 (very light pearl grey).

6 When stitching the star motifs, first stitch the large upright cross and the bars at the end of each arm. Next, stitch the large diagonal cross and the bars at the end of each arm. Lastly, stitch the smaller diagonal cross at the centre.

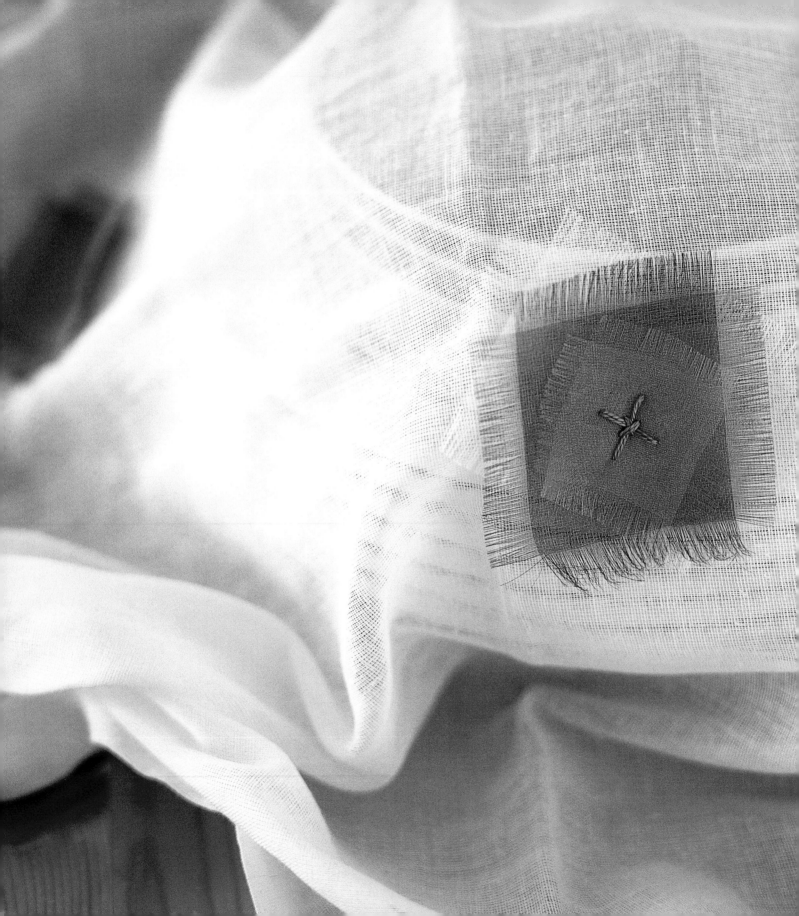

Table throw

A sheer covering of lightweight fabric will keep insects away from an outdoor table setting, allowing preparations to be completed well before the guests arrive.

Voile, organza or fine muslin fabrics are perfect for this project: contrasting patches with frayed edges are attached with large cross stitches to create a stunning effect, taking only a few minutes of your time.

Materials

A piece of cotton muslin or similar, as long as it is wide; for example 1.4 m (55 in) of fabric 140 cm (55 in) wide, or 1.5 metres (59 in) of fabric 150 cm (59 in) wide

Small amounts of silk organza in two or three contrasting colours (in the pictured example, the organza patches are cream, coffee and steel blue)

DMC pearl cotton No 8, to attach the organza patches (in the pictured example, coffee-coloured thread 841 is used)

Tools

Straw hand-sewing needle

4 fabric weights (available from furnishing stores); or use coins

step one Draw a thread along all four sides of the piece of muslin to ensure you have a true square.

step one continued Cut along the drawn thread line.

Laundering

If you need to wash an embroidered piece, do so by hand using cold water and wool detergent or very diluted laundry detergent. Rinse well, then roll in a clean towel to get rid of excess water; never wring the fabric. Allow to dry completely, then press on the wrong side, using a pressing cloth.

Beaded embroidery can be dry-cleaned; or launder as above, then when dry, lay it face down on a thick towel and press from the wrong side.

1 Draw a thread along all four edges of the muslin to ensure you have a true square, then cut along the drawn thread line.

2 Press a double 3 cm (1¼ in) hem along all four sides. Add a weight to each corner, pin the hem into place, then machine stitch the hem 2 mm (¹⁄₁₆ in) from the inner edge.

3 You are now ready to place the organza patches into position. To prepare the patches, cut about 15 pieces of organza in each colour, approximately 6 x 5 cm (2½ x 2 in). Cut them freehand, as they do not all have to be exactly the same size; some variation in size adds to the effect. Fray

step two Place a weight in each corner of the cloth before machine stitching the hem.

step five Pin the organza patches into place, spacing them randomly and varying the order of the colours within the patches, then stitch down with a large cross stitch.

along all four sides of each piece for about 1 cm (⅜ in).

4 Make the patches into groups, giving some groups two layers and others three layers, and arranging the colours in different orders throughout the groups. Place each patch at an angle to the previous, to allow all the colours to show at the edge of the group.

5 Place the groups of patches onto the completed muslin throw. If you wish, lay the throw on a flat surface, such as the floor, so that you can rearrange the patches until you are pleased with the total effect. Pin

them in place, then stitch them down using one or two thicknesses of pearl thread. On each patch, first work a single large uneven cross stitch; if the stitch size floats too much, secure the centre with a smaller upright cross stitch as pictured on page 102. Be sure to start and finish securely so that the stitching can withstand laundering.

Jar covers

Reminiscent of country fairs and school fetes, these simple adornments can turn a jar of homemade preserves into a gift of love. Make these little mob caps from scraps of fabric and thread to personalize jars of produce for your own pantry shelves or to give to someone else.

Muslin or other lightweight cotton fabrics are easy to work with and give a crisp, clean look to the finished jar covers. You can decorate them with abstract designs and simple cross stitches or go to town with threads and embellishments of your choice.

Materials
100 per cent cotton muslin or voile
Leather thonging
Silk cord
Flower thread (the pictured examples use very
  dark salmon pink)
DMC tapestry wool (the pictured examples use
  7110, medium garnet)
DMC pearl cotton No 8, shade 3860

Tools
Compass
Water-soluble fabric marker
  or tailor's chalk
Embroidery scissors
Dressmaking scissors
Elastic bands
Mixed packet crewel hand-sewing needles